soul survival guide

because there are more questions than answers

ali davenport

Published by Ali Davenport

ISBN: 978-1-9164542-1-7

This book is not a substitute for and not to be relied on for medical, healthcare or other professional advice on specific circumstances and in specific locations. Please consult your doctor before changing, stopping or starting any medical treatment. The author disclaims, as far as the law allows, any liability arising directly or indirectly from the use, or misuse, of the information contained in this book.

contents

preface

When I open a non-fiction book, I like to learn something about the writer. A book doesn't appear out of thin air. The author has been inspired to write it and I like to know why. So here is some background for those of you who would like to know my reasons for writing this guide.

I have always been curious about who we are and our place in the universe. Even as a child, I looked up at the stars. I had so many questions – and I'm still asking them.

I was brought up, informally, as a Christian. I enjoyed bible stories and singing hymns, and it gave me my moral base. But at the age of fourteen I stopped believing in God, and this left a hole that I spent a long time trying to fill.

Around the age of forty, I went through the toughest time of my life so far. I'd lived with spells of depression and anxiety from a young age. I didn't like being that way but tried to accept it as part of who I was. I could see that other people had much more to deal with. But my circumstances proved so challenging, it brought a black cloud that hung over my life for two years. In my darker moments, I thought about ending it.

Like a lot of people, I turned to the spiritual and psychological world for answers. It was a pick and mix approach: classes, therapies, and a growing pile of books. They promised solutions but while some of it helped, it often made me feel worse. It was bewildering. Was I lacking in some way, not open enough to new ways of thinking? Why couldn't I be as sure about life as the experts and gurus seemed to be?

In the end, I got through. It was doggedness as much as anything. I clawed my way out of the pit with gritted teeth. This gave me the belief that while support from other people is important, it is ultimately up to us. We have to put ourselves in the driving seat, not be a passenger in our own lives.

The blackest times may have passed but the challenges still come my way. I may be more emotionally intelligent and wiser in my thinking but I don't automatically know what to do for the best. I still get it wrong.

I haven't written this book as someone with all the answers. I'm a traveller, not an expert. I can't say do this and do that and such and such will happen. There are only possibilities.

I do know what it's like to scour around for solutions, wondering which roads to take. I wish there had a been a book like this. One that gave me some idea about where the signposts might be directing me. One that also suggested ways of looking after myself on the journey or at least made me aware it was something to think about. At the same time, it wouldn't ask me to take on a set of beliefs or live a certain way. It would leave it to me to work it out for myself.

This is the book.

welcome

Life is beautiful but tough. The question is, how to get better at surviving it?

The *soul survival guide* can help you find possible answers to that question. It asks you to challenge your thinking and look afresh at old or accepted ideas.

It won't try to persuade you into viewing the world a particular way, nor will it tell you how to live your life. That's up to you. But it will give you some idea of the roads you want to take.

It won't answer your big questions either. Just encourage you to get used to the idea that there are more questions than answers.

Life doesn't go in a straight line. Likewise, the *soul survival guide* doesn't have to be read from start to finish. It has been put together in a way that encourages you to dip in and out as you please.

It is also a book to come to back to. Few of us digest everything at a first reading. It's only when we return – weeks, months, or years down the line – that parts of it resonate in a way they didn't before. We think, 'Ah, I get that now'.

Or we find we've changed our minds. It's one of the joys of life. Nothing is set in stone.

1 staying grounded

In the rush of everyday life, we can quickly get out of kilter with ourselves and the world around us. This first chapter looks at how to stay grounded. It explores ways of bringing ourselves back to balance and how self-reliance helps us stand firm.

both feet on the ground

Grounded people are steady. They don't get caught up in the swirl of powerful emotions and experiences – or if they do, they know how to bring themselves back. They have a secure sense of who they are, taking other people's views on board but not being led by them. They see the wider picture and make rational decisions based on evidence. They don't get carried away by pipe dreams or unrealistic expectations.

Being grounded doesn't mean being over-serious and sensible. In many ways, it allows for lightness and a sense of exploration. When there's a stable centre to come back to, we can go with the flow. Someone who travels from place to place can be as grounded as the person who lives in the same town all their life. It's a way of being that goes with us wherever we are.

applying the brakes

We all know that constantly rushing around isn't good for us. But it's all too easy to become the proverbial headless chicken.

Consciously applying the brakes gives us more control. This doesn't mean going at a snail's pace, just reducing the rate. Few of us would take a bend at ninety miles an hour, so why go at life like that? It's counter-productive. When we're harassed or tired, we're more likely to waste mental energy and make mistakes. It can also have a negative effect on our relationships. People who create flurry aren't always easy to be around.

Doing things in a more measured way gives the body more time to breathe and the brain more time to think.

sorting out priorities

There are only so many hours in the day. With the best will in the world, we can't fit in everything we need, or want, to do. Something has to give – which means making choices.

It might be time to sit down and take a look at your priorities. Write a list and organise it into what you absolutely have to do, what can wait, and what you could lose all together. Take care not to sacrifice activities that nurture you and give you enjoyment.

It may feel like a puzzle without a solution - there are just too many demands on your time - but you have to find a way of making it work. The alternative is to continue as you are, which could have a long-term impact on your health and wellbeing. You'll function less well and achieve less with the time you have.

Sometimes we're stuck in a mindset where we're convinced that everything is equally important and has to be squashed in one way or another. Perhaps you've become hostage to high standards or ideals about how life should be. Housework is a prime example. Does it really matter if the bedsheets aren't ironed or the dusting is left for a few days? Maybe you're trying to be a superhero. Can other people share some of the responsibility?

Use creative thinking to look at your routines and how you do tasks. Perhaps your days could be organised more effectively? Can you make one journey instead of two or find a piece of equipment that gets a job done faster?

Most importantly, build in downtime. We all need it, more so when we're in overdrive. This could be half an hour to sit with your feet up or to have a nap. It's a necessity, not a treat.

when you're losing your footing

We often become ungrounded over a period of time. Try to notice if this is happening. There may be feelings of unease, something you can't quite put your finger on. Perhaps you're more emotional than usual or doubting your ability to cope with so many demands. You might feel disconnected, even adrift, as if your life isn't your own anymore.

Being alert to when you're going off course means you can take action to bring yourself back. Find activities that re-ground you. This might be getting in touch with nature, spending time with family, or playing music. It isn't self-indulgent. Doing stuff that makes us feel good about ourselves and the world is vital to our wellbeing. It helps maintain our equilibrium, so we're less likely to go off-kilter in the first place.

doing away with the drama

A fast-track to turbulence is to create or get involved in drama. It can quickly propel us off centre, with the effects lasting for weeks or months.

Dramas happen when our emotions take over. We jump in, losing our perspective and making mountains out of molehills. Step back. Give yourself time to cool down so you're not as agitated, distressed or angry. You may even find it isn't as big a deal as you first thought.

While it isn't always possible to avoid dramas, we can limit our participation. There may be sparks but we don't have to catch them!

keeping it real

Having dreams is part of being human. They motivate us and give us hope. If we don't keep a check on them though, they become fantasies, leaving us frustrated and unfulfilled.

We can be grounded and still dream. Just remember, life has a way of panning out in unexpected ways. Goal posts shift, and we have to adjust our sights or aim for something else. Even if our dreams do come true, the reality may be very different to what we imagined.

If we do achieve success, it's important to keep our feet on the ground. Being swept along and losing ourselves can leave us floundering if our fortunes turn.

the road to self-reliance

An essential part of being grounded is a solid sense of self-reliance. This doesn't mean living like a hermit. It's having robust inner resources to deal with whatever life brings rather than being a feather for every wind.

Take someone with a serious illness. They may have all kinds of support from their medical team, family, friends and partner, but in the end, they are the ones who have to go through it. Someone who becomes very dependent in this situation will struggle.

Not everyone is brought up in a way that nurtures self-reliance, but it can be developed. Spending time on your own regularly is a good place to start. Try going for a walk or visiting somewhere like a coffee shop or the cinema. It isn't a sign of social failure. There may be people who feel sorry for you, but it says more about them than you. Equally, there may be others admiring you, wishing they had the courage to do it.

Another way to develop self-sufficiency is to tackle those tasks you'd rather avoid. You've let other people sort out your household bills or make those tricky phone calls. As well as making you dependent, it reinforces your inadequacy. Trust your amazing human capacity to learn. It probably means stepping out of your comfort zone, but little by little, you can build up your confidence – and self-esteem with it.

A key area for self-reliance is what we do when problems come up. We often dive for the phone, calling friends and family. But this can make things worse, especially if they are connected to the problem. They may not say what we want to hear or offer the sympathy we expect. Grounded people seek their own counsel first. They listen to what others have to say, but they don't look to others to tell them what to do. They also try not to load their troubles on other people's shoulders – or at least keep it to a minimum.

The road to self-reliance brings rewards. There is nothing like that sense of being anchored whatever the winds of life bring.

2 living with limits

The idea of going beyond our limits is an enticing one. There is a huge universe out there, waiting to be explored. Who needs boundaries? Surely the true soul-searcher can do without them?

bound from birth

Whether we like it or not, there are limits on us from birth. There are the genes we inherit, and the culture and religion of the society we are born into. We have clock time and the counting of years, multiple systems, and codes of moral and social behaviour. There is nothing we can do about it. It's just how it is. Boundaries are part and parcel of life.

If we were stranded on a desert island, the likelihood is we would create some kind of structure in our day. Even the most non-conformist among us have routines and ways of doing things. Not to say we are hard and fast creatures, but we all have parameters. When these break down, as in the case of severe mental illness, our ability to participate in the world reduces or ceases all together. Boundaries keep us pinned to life.

freedom within borders

It's a joy to throw away the rulebook and think outside the box. But the pleasure comes from having a rulebook in the first place, a box to step out of. We don't exist in a vacuum. Too much freedom can be inhibiting, like the classic Blank Page Syndrome. The writer stares at the empty page, completely paralysed by choice.

Limitations can be a spur, fuelling rather than hampering creativity. We have to think around problems, approaching from different angles. This encourages us to experiment and innovate.

Life shows us many examples where freedom is found within boundaries. Take the Buddhist whose strict meditative practice allows them to explore different levels of consciousness or the ballet dancer who rehearses rigorously to reach something beautiful and free-flowing in performance. What these have in common is disciplined practice. The supporting structures provide the platform to freedom.

learning from the professionals

If there's any aspect of life where we need boundaries, it's in our relationships, especially if we're a carer or supporting someone. Health and social care professions have strict guidelines and codes of behaviour to protect staff and the people they work with. We can learn from these to apply to our personal lives:

a buffer against burnout

Few people can provide constant care on tap without it affecting their wellbeing. Professional boundaries recognise this and help to deal with the drain on inner resources.

Professionals give themselves permission to cut off. They know that if they carry their work around with them, they risk becoming overwhelmed or having compassion fatigue. What matters is the support given in the moment, not what happens after it.

When we're caring for someone, there's a danger of becoming completely absorbed by it, exhausting ourselves in the process. Guilt is often the culprit, making us feel bad for not always having the other person at the forefront of our minds. But it's vital to have time out, to lay our efforts aside for a while.

not being taken advantage of

Sometimes professionals come across clients who try to take advantage of the relationship. This is why there are guidelines, like not giving personal contact details or accepting gifts. They prevent lines getting blurred.

A professional sets time limits with clients. If they find themselves doing more and more for a person, especially out of usual working hours, it's a sure sign they are crossing boundaries.

It can be helpful to restrict the amount of time you give to someone. If you are visiting a demanding family member to give support, put a time limit on it in advance, and stick to it. They don't have to know you are doing it. Likewise, it might be time to talk to someone about their habit of calling you late at night.

Without realising it, we can allow people to emotionally blackmail us. We may end up doing more and more for an elderly neighbour even though they have family locally who can look after them. It is being clear about what you will and will not do and, while it isn't easy, standing firm.

Establishing boundaries reduces the risk of overload and means your support is likely to be of a better quality.

guarding against saviour behaviour

It's tempting for professionals to rush in to rescue their clients. But playing the superhero is never helpful. Rather than empowering people to deal with their problems, it creates dependency, or they feel stifled and want to break away.

Swooping in to rescue friends and family comes from the right place, but if there is any saving to be done, it has to be by the person themselves. We can play our part in supporting them, but it's the stuff of fantasy to think we can fly in and solve all their problems.

Another version of saviour behaviour is climbing into the ditch with someone. This is when we think we have to go through every step with them. It's harder to help a person out of the ditch if we're in there with them – and we might get stuck there ourselves!

not putting people on a pedestal

Working within boundaries reminds professionals not to idealise clients. Everyone is an individual with their faults and flaws, and going through difficulties doesn't make a person saintly. They need support not reverence.

We see this with sick children when people say 'You're so brave' or 'What a little soldier'. Heroic labels like this put pressure on people. They feel they have to put on a front to live up to expectations. Much better to provide support and care in a way that allows them to take the mask off.

setting standards of behaviour

Professional guidelines set the baseline for acceptable behaviour. If a client becomes aggressive or violent, staff can let them know it won't be tolerated and have consequences if it continues.

It's a much greyer area in our personal relationships. We tend to give more leeway or make excuses. We may even question ourselves, wondering if we're over-reacting or expecting too much.

While it isn't an easy subject to broach, boundaries can be put in place. It means naming the behaviour for what it is and letting the person know it isn't acceptable to you. This doesn't mean you don't care. In the wider picture, you may be doing more harm than good by allowing the behaviour to continue.

On occasion, a client's behaviour deteriorates to the point where the professional relationship ends. This can happen in personal relationships too. Sometimes the best course is to bring it to a close.

boundaries as back up

There are people in the mind, spirit and body world who operate within very loose boundaries. Some are con-merchants, motivated by money, power and sex. Their prey is often the most vulnerable, like the bereaved or seriously ill. Less obvious are the ones who believe they have special powers or purpose. They are often charismatic and high up in their field: gurus, masters or teachers. This authority allows them to gain trust easily and makes it difficult to question them, especially if surrounded by devotees.

We may be more susceptible to this kind of person at difficult times in our lives. Like Hansel and Gretel, we start guzzling in the spiritual sweetshop, forgetting there might be the equivalent of the hag in the house.

Keeping the edges blurry makes it easier for these people to ask us to do something we may not be sure of. This is why it's important to have a safe and supported environment, whatever the practice or therapy. You should be able to opt out at any time and for that decision to be respected. Be wary of someone who says 'Trust me' or 'Trust the process' and makes you feel it's your fault if their therapy doesn't work – they claim you're too resistant or have some kind of 'blockage'. It may just be that a different practice or practitioner would suit you better.

Before you commit to mind, spirit and body experiences, research them, especially the more extreme. Don't be afraid of asking questions. If the organisers don't reply or give vague answers, it could be a warning sign.

Think about what you would do if you want to withdraw from an activity. Are you prepared to be assertive, even if pressure is being put on you? It may bring up difficult feelings or affect you badly. Do you have ideas for taking care of yourself and an exit strategy if needed?

Boundaries like this act as a back-up, so we're not free-falling without a parachute.

3 when relationships turn toxic

We all know toxic relationships should be avoided. But it is easy to get caught up in them. This chapter takes a look at these relationships when it is the other person bringing the poison.

the warning signs
We're not always aware how unhealthy a relationship is. We might be blinded by romantic love or our hopes for a new friendship. Perhaps we're used to it being that way and haven't noticed how bad it has become.

There are always signs that a relationship has turned toxic or is heading that way. There is usually some kind of imbalance. They're demanding of you and use emotional blackmail to keep you in line. This is often accompanied by bullying, eroding your confidence and self-esteem. You don't want to upset them, so you avoid arguments. If you do raise concerns about their behaviour, you're likely to be dismissed. It might even be put back onto you, so you feel at fault and find yourself apologising.

We often make excuses for the person: they had a bad childhood, it's their health condition, deep down they love us. We scramble around for small scraps of evidence to justify the relationship. But when it comes down it, nothing justifies persistent poor behaviour.

grasping the nettle
One of the most direct ways of dealing with a toxic relationship is to talk to the person. But this comes with a warning. The unhealthy patterns have usually set in by the time you do this, so it can blow back in your face.

A measured approach is best. Be calm, not confrontational. Toxic people feed on distress and unease. It shows they have power over you. Staying neutral gives them less to knock against.

If you can't talk to them, try making changes in a subtle way. If they are used to you dropping everything to be with them, take a little longer to respond each time. They may not realise it's happening, or if they do, it isn't drastic enough for them to jump on you for it. It can take persistence, especially if the dynamics have been that way for a long time, but it's possible to slowly shift the balance.

We often allow bad relationships to eat up our energy. Pay attention to yourself instead, doing activities to build up your self-esteem and sense of worth. The relationship may not change, but it'll have less impact on you.

While ending a relationship is difficult, sometimes it is the only option. Their reaction may be ugly, but let them vent. It's often confirmation you are doing the right thing.

fools rush in

Toxic relationships are like potholes, they trip us up unexpectedly. But if we watch where we're going, we can spot them in good time.

Try not to hurtle into a new friendship or romantic relationship. Take time to get to know the person. If something jars, don't be too quick to dismiss it. Alarm bells generally go off for a reason.

There is a major advantage to giving a relationship breathing space. It might set it off on a different dynamic, preventing it from turning toxic in the first place.

Resist the urge to rescue someone, flying in like a superhero to save them from their problems or personality shortfalls. They may be going through something you have experienced, but it's not your job to swoop in and steer them through depression or a bad divorce. Pulling on the superhero pants is never helpful, and toxic people can turn unexpectedly. It doesn't matter how caring and supportive you might be; the kinder you are, the quicker they can switch.

closing the door to energy vampires

The vampire of fiction can't enter a person's home without being invited. This is a good metaphor to think about in terms of protecting ourselves from energy vampires. It's often our own behaviour that allows them to gain entry. We open the door and let them in.

They can be needy creatures, looking up to us – at least at the beginning. Something about us attracts them, often what they lack themselves, like our vitality or emotional strength. It makes us feel good, and we quickly take them under our wing.

Sometimes we're disarmed by what seems to be a special bond. In no time at all they have become a best friend, in constant contact and privy to our thoughts. We may enjoy this intensity at first, but it sets a pattern. They become enmeshed in our lives, so when we turn away to do other things they feel left out in the cold. In vampire terms, this is understandable. After feeding daily off the relationship, the food source runs dry. They hunger for more, becoming jealous of other people in our lives.

Energy vampires are often emotionally demanding. Some love drama and need us as their audience. Watching them crash from one drama to another, we begin to wonder about the ex-partner or friend they are always criticizing. Perhaps it wasn't as one-sided as it seems.

If you want to end the relationship, beware – energy vampires tend not to retreat quietly. They go for the jugular. An alternative is to disengage in small steps, weaning them off. Gradually reduce the amount of contact, and don't respond to them as quickly when they call you. With luck, they'll lose interest and go off to find another victim.

An advantage of this staggered approach is that it may get to the point where it becomes a healthier relationship, one to be enjoyed rather than avoided.

4 the ache of invisible bruises

Emotional abuse can happen to anyone and in any kind of relationship. This chapter focuses on romantic relationships. How do we break the cycle and start to heal?

signs of emotional abuse

If some of these signs seem familiar, you may be in an emotionally abusive relationship or one that is heading that way.

Your partner belittles you and puts you down. This might be privately, in front of other people, or both. While they may not be loud or aggressive, their words feel like pinches or punches. It makes you flinch and shrink into yourself.

They seem to enjoy unsettling and upsetting you, whether it's driving too fast, flirting with others in front of you, or tying you in knots during arguments. They may be controlling, monitoring what you wear and where you go, and accusing you of things you haven't done.

You walk on eggshells, afraid of doing or saying something that sparks a response. You're increasingly passive for the sake of peace. At the same time, you try to please them; their approval or disapproval can make or spoil your day.

If you tell them how you're feeling, they turn it around so you feel to blame. You may even find yourself apologising. They're always able to justify their behaviour: they had a tough childhood, they're under stress at work, their behaviour is nothing like it used to be. This makes you feel bad for challenging them about it.

You question yourself, wondering if you're being over-sensitive or expecting too much. You try to work out what you can do to make it better.

the slow hurt

Emotional abuse is far less obvious than physical abuse. It creeps into relationships. Each incident may be small and not seem a great deal in itself but added together it becomes abuse.

It wears us down without our realising, eroding our self-esteem and ability to stand up for ourselves.

Anyone can find themselves in an abusive relationship. The first step in defence is acknowledging that it could happen to you. If something jars in a new relationship, don't dismiss it. It can be put in a mental drawer, but at least it hasn't been ignored.

It helps to have boundaries around behaviour. Friendly jibing is one thing but what if it regularly tips into belittling? If you raise it with them and they're dismissive, mocking even, you have to seriously question whether it is the best relationship for you.

If you're constantly giving them the benefit of the doubt, then something isn't right. People can always find a way to justify their poor behaviour. Don't be blind-sided by their being in a caring profession or having great relationships with family and friends. You might be the only person they're like that with, but it's still abuse.

They may have acknowledged past behaviour and be making efforts to change. This is sometimes used as an excuse to continue with it. They tell you they are much better than they used to be, they're trying their best, give them a break. Watch you're not being manipulated this way. They may not even realise they are doing it.

Sometimes we put too much faith in the power of love. Deep down they must care for us, they just don't know how to show it. If we meet their abuse with care and understanding, they'll soften in the end. Sadly, this is often more of a wish than reality. Love doesn't always win the day.

breaking the vicious cycle

Lenore Edna Walker developed the idea of The Cycle of Abuse in the 1970s. Tensions build in the first phase, leading to an outburst of abuse in the acting out phase. The honeymoon period sees reconciliation, followed by a period of calm before tensions start to build again.

While Walker's cycle relates to physical abuse, emotional abuse can follow a similar pattern. It's draining to go through it again and again. At a lower ebb each time, there are less inner resources to draw on. Wounds haven't healed, so scabs come off quickly.

It can take a long time to realise you are in the cycle. It becomes the norm, just the way it is. You cling on, hoping for a change that never comes. In the end, the cycle has to be broken. Unfortunately, severing contact on a permanent basis tends to be the only way of doing this.

healing the wounds

The damage from emotional abuse can take a long time to heal. It's a diminishing experience, robbing us of wellbeing and self-worth.

You may be suffering from depression or anxiety, even suicidal feelings, so it is important to have professional support. Talking to friends and family can help but choose people who won't judge you. You don't need to hear 'I told you so' or be made to feel that it's your own fault. Someone more independent, like a counsellor, is often better at this stage. They won't downplay or dismiss your experience.

As you start to recover, you may become aware of strong feelings of anger. These are often buried along the way and only re-surface in the aftermath. It's important to give expression to these feelings rather than pushing them back down. There are ways to vent safely, whether it's crying, thumping a pillow, or writing it down. You're not hurting anyone and it helps to get it out of your system.

Don't feel you have to forgive the person or seek reconciliation at this stage. Your good grace is unlikely to bring the desired result and may well throw you back into the cycle. It can wait – and you never have to mend bridges if you don't want to.

It isn't wise to rush into another relationship. Your emotional resources will be low, making you vulnerable. Sadly, some people crash from one abusive relationship into the next. You may have been a victim this time, but you don't have to be forever.

5 the darker shores of the soul

Hopelessness and despair lie on the darker shores. Many of us visit this lonely place during our lives, with some never returning. This chapter explores those farthest reaches and how to make our way back if we find ourselves there.

falling into the pit

For some it is a sudden drop, others a slow slide. Whichever way, the pit is a deep and lonely place. Little light makes its way in and sometimes disappears altogether.

People tell us we are not alone, but this brings little comfort. It only confirms that the world is full of pain. Or it makes us feel guilty – life is a gift, and we are wasting it.

Mental health isn't like other illness. How much is us and how much the condition? It's hard to tell where it begins and ends. The chemical and neurological aspects are only one side of the story, part of the interplay between how we were brought up, the way we think, and where we are in our lives.

No single treatment is going to make everything all right. This places a large onus on the individual. While support from others is crucial, it's ultimately down to us – and this makes it daunting. The steps to self-help can feel like hurdles, with the ever-present risk of being knocked back. Added to this, local mental health services are often over-stretched. With everything against us like this, why not just stay in the pit? Well, we can of course. We can stay there for as long as we like. Or we can opt out. Sometimes suicide seems to be the only choice.

when you want to cut the rope

The statistics are staggering. Up to a million people in the world take their own lives each year, with many more attempting it. Despite this, it's still a taboo subject.

The truth is, life sometimes feels too much to bear. Thrown onto the darker shores, suicide can seem the best option, a rational choice even. It's not that we want to die, we want the pain and struggle to end.

The taboo makes it difficult to express suicidal thoughts, but talking about them reduces their power. If you are having thoughts about ending your life, please call The Samaritans or similar service. It can be a life-saver – literally – offering the kind of non-judgemental support which is often difficult for loved ones to give. You don't have to wait until you are on the verge of suicide or in the middle of an attempt. They are there to talk to at any time. Expressing your darkest thoughts to someone neutral but compassionate can bring a huge sense of relief and may well be the turning point.

There are millions of people living happy and healthy lives who have considered suicide. There is something potentially liberating about going to that far shore and standing on the cusp between life and death. The trick, of course, is coming back from it; looking death square in the face but choosing life.

climbing back out

When we're at the bottom of the pit, it seems impossible to get out of it. But there are hand and footholds to help us. It's just that we can't always see them, especially at the beginning. Like a climber, we have to feel about, finding places to take hold to help ourselves up.

Everyone's climb is different and it may take a long time, but every inch upwards is a move in the right direction. You can also make a safety net as you go along, so the drop behind you isn't as far.

Here are some ideas to get you started:

self-compassion and more self-compassion

If you are experiencing emotional pain, please show yourself compassion. It doesn't matter how you got there. You may have been selfish or made poor choices, but that can be worked through later. Never mind that other people seem to be worse off – it doesn't take anything away from your experience. The pit is a terrible place to find yourself in and being kind to yourself is crucial.

weathering it out

Weathering is an opportunity to be with ourselves as we truly are, taking off the mask to allow difficult emotions to pass through. It's like being a sailor, alone on a boat as a storm approaches, sitting tight to weather it out.

It takes practice to weather effectively. You don't have to do it for long, and you can stop at any point if it gets too much.

Hunker down in an environment that feels safe and secure. Close the curtains, light candles, make a huddle of blankets – whatever works for you. Avoid alcohol or anything that will cloud or over-heighten the experience.

Allow the storm to come, without censoring any of it or pushing it down. Let it be as it is, in all its rawness. You might lie still with your eyes closed or move about. Do what you need to do to help it pass through.

Afterwards, it helps to sleep or rest. Above all, be kind to yourself.

It takes courage to face the worst but weathering like this teaches us that the unbearable is bearable. We can come through it and survive.

dropping the mask

As a society, we are talking about mental health more than ever. But many of us still feel the shame, keeping it hidden from work colleagues, our social circle and loved ones. We pretend that everything is okay or at least not as bad as it really is.

Constantly covering up is hard work, draining resources that are already low. Maybe it's time to hold up your hands and say, 'I'm struggling here'. It often brings immediate relief and is a turning point for many people. Your energies can go into getting better instead.

asking for help

Few people come through the worst times in their lives without any kind of professional support. Your doctor is usually the best place to start. They often suggest medication, which can seem too easy a solution and not really dealing your problems, but it has its place. It's worth considering, even if just for a temporary period.

Your doctor is the gateway to a range of therapies, Cognitive Behavioural Therapy (CBT) often being the most available. This helps you challenge unhelpful thought patterns and core beliefs that affect the way you see the world. These aren't easily unpicked, however. CBT often has to be revisited over a period of time, making it a learning process rather than a quick fix.

Many people find counselling helpful. This is a talking therapy, typically for a block of six to ten sessions. Counsellors don't tell you how to fix things; you work it out for yourself with their support. It doesn't suit everyone, but sometimes it's down to lack of rapport with the counsellor or events may still be too close. Unfortunately, there are often long waiting lists, although there may be free counselling in your area targeted at particular groups, such as the under 25s.

Groups are a great source of support at little or no cost. They are usually run by health professionals or volunteers connected to a national organisation or local health service. The approach varies; it might be sharing personal experiences, socialising, or discussing a different topic each time.

Going to a first meeting can be daunting, especially if your confidence is low. It helps to contact the organiser beforehand to smooth the way. Perhaps you can take a friend or be matched with a buddy until you've settled in.

Courses and activities are another form of group support. This might be confidence-building, arts and crafts, gardening or mindfulness. There are also self-management courses, like the Expert Patient Programme, to build up coping strategies and resilience. Your doctor won't always know what's on offer, so have a search on the internet or contact local mental health services for signposting.

There is always online support, which can be accessed anonymously from your own home at any time of the day or night. You can read forums and blogs, or get more involved by sharing your story and posting comments. It's a way of connecting with people around the world who are going through similar experiences. It's often comforting to know you are not alone.

don't wait until you feel like it

One of the cardinal rules of self-management is not to wait until you feel like doing something. That feeling can take a long time in coming, if at all.

Doing nothing all day rarely makes us feel better. We have to find a way through the inertia, however uncomfortable it is – and on a daily basis. Do some tidying, take a short walk, keep that appointment. Poor mental health gives us all kinds of reasons why we shouldn't bother, but it is only by the doing that we have any chance of moving forward.

Be aware that you may not always feel better for your efforts. Your state of mind may cloud your perception so you don't feel a change in mood. The way to approach it is to think, 'Okay, I don't feel any different but it is probably doing me good'.

Better to do something rather than nothing. At the very least, it breaks the day up and helps you get through the hours.

the stepping stones to self-belief

Mental illness often leaves huge dents in our self-confidence, when we may not have had much to begin with.

The way to build confidence and self-esteem is to take it steady and not overwhelm yourself. When we're at a low ebb, our negative thoughts are all too ready to dive in if we over-challenge ourselves. They tell us there is no point in trying, it's only going to end in failure.

Take small steps, building up slowly. If your goal is to get out of the house, walk to the end of your road on the first day, to the local shop on the second, and the park on the third. You'll feel a greater sense of achievement, and it's easier to shake off the disappointment if you miss the odd target.

Recording what you've done gives you something to look back on. Seeing how far we've come often gives us a boost. It's also evidence that confidence can be developed from wherever we are.

turning tunnel vision around

When we're in the pit, it feels as if life will always be that way. We get tunnel vision and forget the times when we felt more positive about life.

A way round this is to be less absolute. When we divide our lives into 'bad days' and 'good days', there is only the option of one or the other. In reality, life is a flow and there are constant fluctuations, some of them very subtle.

However awful you feel, it's unlikely to stay at the same level all day. There will be times when it lessens, and these small chinks are like finger-holes in the pit wall. Try to be aware of them. The hope is that they become longer and increase in number as you recover, until the balance tips and the world generally feels brighter.

Another way of being less black and white, is to insert the word 'probably' into your thinking. Tell yourself that it will probably get better – or at least, it probably won't always be as bad.

fending off the guilt goblin

The Guilt Goblin likes to dig its claws into our shoulders: What have we got to complain about? How can we can be so ungrateful and self-centred? What a fraud!

Unfortunately, telling yourself not to feel guilty rarely banishes the Goblin. The most effective way of showing it the back door is doing things to help yourself get better. When we do nothing, its grip gets stronger. Activity gives it less to hang onto and helps to combat the feelings of worthlessness. It also reduces the anxiety of those close to you. They are probably afraid of you sinking further into the hole, so it's reassuring to see you doing things to help yourself out of it.

owning the illness

Depression and despair are often seen as a Black Dog or other dark force. It looms large in our lives, coming and going as it wishes. Even when we are well, there is always the threat of it returning.

We tend not to view other health conditions in the same way. Someone with diabetes has to monitor and manage their blood sugar to stay well. It's part of their daily life. They know it can fluctuate and that certain behaviours will have a detrimental effect.

Taking the same approach to mental health means we're less likely to see ourselves at the mercy of some beast. It's a condition to be managed, and the way we do that directly impacts on our quality of life. This makes us much more active participants in our treatment and recovery.

It allows more room for our uniqueness. A group of people with a mental health condition may share some common symptoms, but this doesn't mean they are all the same. What helps one person doesn't automatically help another. By working out what's best for us, we can own the illness rather than the illness owning us.

good for the soul

On the darker shores, we're often removed from the uplifting stuff that makes us feel good about being alive. We see the world from behind glass, and it's a grey and joyless place to be.

But now and then, however briefly, a few rays of light find their way in. Try to notice when this happens and make a note of what caused it. The idea is to identify what makes you feel good, then generate more of it. It could be the simplest of things, like looking at a favourite photograph or hearing a particular song. These are your pearls. They may not shed much light at the beginning, but the more you gather, the greater the glow.

Thankfulness is another way to nourish yourself. Writing down a couple of things you're thankful for each day is proven to have positive benefits. This might be in a diary or something more creative, like dropping scraps of paper into a jar and watching it build up over the days and months. The trick is to capture the smaller stuff, specific to that day.

Of course, when we're at our worst, it can be a struggle to find things to be thankful for. It's always something you can come back to later.

unearthing riches on the darker shore

Going to the furthest reaches of ourselves has the potential to shape us in ways we never expected. Finding our way back takes tenacity, a determination not to give up. There's inner strength to be found, a resilience we never knew we had. This is why people can see their bad times as a gift.

Suffering can widen our experience of what it is to be human, increasing our compassion for others and making us better people. It may also give us a new appreciation of life. The air feels so good out of the pit.

6 tending the fire

Anger is a very human emotion. Whether it's everyday annoyances or outrage at the wider world, few of us avoid the lick of its flames. The problems start when it gets out of control and ruins relationships and lives.

heeding the red flags

Anger doesn't erupt out of the blue. It waves warning flags, but we often don't notice – or choose to ignore them.

While anger is felt as an emotion, it has a very real physical effect on the body. The instinctive 'fight, flight or freeze' response kicks in, flooding the body with hormones. We breathe faster, clenching our muscles as we prepare for action. Clear thinking takes a back seat, giving anger room to play.

We can develop our ability to pick up on these physical flags, using the information they give us. This helps to keep control at the front of the brain, regulating our behaviour.

Try to notice the changes in your body. The jaw is one of the first areas to be affected. Has it tightened, making your voice shriller and sharper? Are you breathing at a faster rate? Have your body movements become erratic?

Other flags come from the people around you. Are they backing off? Have they asked you to calm down or observed that you're getting wound up? If this acts like a red rag to a bull, it's a clear sign you're going up several gears.

Take heed of your inner voice, the one that tells you not to act rashly. It often gets drowned out as the anger surges, but try to hook onto it and let it pull you back. It's the wiser part of you.

creating firebreaks

Forests have firebreaks, strips of open space to prevent a fire from spreading. We can create our own, making space between the trigger and our response.

Counting to ten is a classic way to do this, but the temptation is to rush or cut it short. Try taking several deep breaths instead.

This has an immediate physical impact, activating the part of the nervous system that calms us down.

When something sparks our anger, our thoughts race along the neural pathways, making connections with past experiences and our core beliefs about the world. Practising mindfulness or a mind management technique, like Cognitive Behavioural Therapy, can help with this. When we're more aware of the rush of automatic thoughts, we can stop ourselves from turning a humdrum event into a drama.

Taking ourselves away is often a wise move. This creates physical as well as psychological space, giving everyone involved a chance to cool off.

recognising the buzz

When we get angry, chemical changes create a rush in our brains. This can be very exciting, pushing the thinking part of us aside and encouraging us to be reckless. We may feel powerful, invincible even, especially if fuelled by a sense of righteousness or alcohol. It gives us permission to behave in ways we wouldn't normally. Regret and shame only come later.

It might seem odd to think of anger as an enjoyable experience but think about the phrases we use – blowing a gasket, flying off the handle, hitting the ceiling. There is a sense of release and freedom. Recognising there may a buzz for you around anger can help you challenge your response.

venting safely

Being angry isn't necessarily the problem – it's what we do with it. There are ways of releasing it without causing physical or emotional damage. We could suppress it, but that doesn't allow our bodies to deal naturally with the hit of hormones, and we might be shoring up psychological problems for the future.

There are ways of venting safely, whether it's doing some vigorous exercise, expressing it in words, or going somewhere to shout alone. None of these hurt anyone or worsen the situation. Meanwhile, it allows the para-sympathetic nervous system to kick in, lowering your heart rate and blood pressure.

Venting to a friend or family member has its drawbacks, especially in the thick of the moment. It may be difficult for them to say the right thing. We might feel like they're lecturing us or taking sides. It's usually wiser to offload to others when we've had time to calm down and think more clearly.

understanding what sparks the blaze

Knowing what triggers your anger gives you more control. Why do some things run off your back while others make you zoom from nought to ninety?

Make a list of situations and events which made you angry. How would you rate the intensity from one to ten? What set you off, and how justified did you feel? Were there any contributing factors, like alcohol or stress? What were your feelings about it afterwards?

Look for patterns. Perhaps the same thing hits your buttons every time, or the angrier you get, the more remorseful you feel afterwards. Reflect on occasions when you dealt successfully with your anger. Why was this the case? If you never handle it well, think about what success would look like.

giving up the blame game

Anger often comes from not feeling enough control over external events. Our world isn't what we want it to be or how we thought it was. It's understandable to feel frustrated, but the lack of control can pass into our own behaviour.

It's easier to blame everyone else for the circumstances in our lives rather than face our own shortcomings. But even if there is good reason to be angry, we have to own our response. Someone's behaviour may have caused our bad mood but it's not their fault if we fly into a rage and do something we regret. That is entirely down to us and not managing ourselves effectively.

facing the demon

Chronic anger is a problem that needs to be dealt with. But it isn't easy to face the ugliness in ourselves and the hurt we have caused. It takes guts to strip the layers back – and persistence. Our patterns of behaviour are often a lifetime in the making and not easily unpicked.

Childhood experiences often have a huge impact. We learn from the adults around us, and anger may have been the norm. Not just arguments and fights but less obvious forms, like passive aggressive behaviour or a sense of tension.

How did anger play out in your family? Did it affect the dynamic between you and other family members? Does it still affect your relationships with them today? As mature an adult as we may be, we can quickly switch back into child mode when our buttons are pressed.

Sometimes chronic anger develops out of life experiences. This could be illness, loss, problems with work or romantic relationships. Although we might not be able to change our circumstances, we can address the way we respond.

Professional input is often needed when anger has rooted itself. The feelings of remorse and self-loathing it can bring up are hard to deal with on your own. Counselling provides a supportive environment to talk about and reflect on experiences, which may include reaching back to your younger years and the events and relationships that shaped you. It can be a cathartic process, allowing you to forgive yourself while taking responsibility for how you live your life in the future.

Anger management courses are available online or there may be groups in your area. While online courses have anonymity, there is something about sitting and sharing experiences with others that can be powerful and transforming.

healing in the ashes

While we can't go back and change how we've behaved in the past, we can start afresh from where we are. Acknowledging the impact our anger has had on those around us is a huge first step. But is only the beginning. Healing is a process and it takes time and effort to mend bridges.

Apologising often isn't enough and may not be received well at first. Your loved ones need to see there is a genuine, long-term commitment to change. Some people justify continued poor behaviour by saying 'But I went for counselling' or 'I'm so much better than I used to be'. Going on a course or reading a book doesn't suddenly fix everything.

One way to promote healing is to give the people you've hurt the opportunity to tell you how your anger has affected them. This has to be taken on the chin, not argued with or excuses made. They need you to really listen to what is said; to allow it and acknowledge it.

In some cases, too much damage has been done and the other person doesn't want reconciliation. You can torture yourself forever with 'if only'. Practising self-compassion can help you find a way to forgive yourself. The past is what it is. The focus is on what happens from this day forward.

weathering someone else's storm

It's tough to be on the receiving end of chronic anger. As much as you try, it's difficult not to be affected. Here are some suggestions for dealing with it:

resisting retaliation

When someone is gunning for a fight, they want a reaction. They'll prod and provoke until you join in the fray.

The path of non-retaliation aims to diffuse the situation rather than add to it. This is more than not arguing back. We can goad the other person with passive aggressive behaviour, such as sulking or stonewalling. People use this to dodge responsibility – 'Well, I didn't get angry' or 'I wasn't the one shouting' – but in reality, they have been an active participant.

Meeting anger with calm and reasoned argument often doesn't work as a strategy. When adrenalin is pumping around the body, people operate from their emotions, not the mind.

The best thing you can do is allow them to vent. Let them have their say and do some acknowledging, such as 'I can see you're very angry' or 'I see that what I have done has upset you.' It can feel odd saying what you see like this, but it works as a technique. You're not judging, apologising or defending; just stating what you see in a neutral way. It shows you are listening. You're not giving your approval but you recognise how they feel.

Sometimes this is all people need to allow them to get it out of their system and calm down.

stepping away from the fire

You always have the right to walk away. A psychological assault can be just as damaging as a physical attack, and there is always the risk it could turn physically violent. They may never have harmed you before, but this could be the time they step over the line.

Unfortunately, they may make it difficult to leave, blocking the doorway or restraining you in some way. If this happens, take some deep breaths, keep your wits about you and try and work out an exit strategy. Allow them to vent as described above.

Don't let guilt keep you locked into the conflict. The person may be angry because of something you've done, but you don't have to take the brunt of it there and then. It doesn't mean you're trying to get out of being held into account, just not at that time. Likewise, they may accuse you of a being a coward or use emotional blackmail to keep you there. How can you abandon them? But at the end of the day, you don't have to stand there and take it. No one should be a punchbag.

in the aftermath

Being on the end of someone's anger can be draining, more so if you haven't retaliated. You're in the flight or fight response but haven't acted on it. This may leave you shaky and emotional.

Try to find a way of safely venting any anger or distress. You might feel guilty for feeling angry, but it's a natural response. It's healthier to let it out rather than bottle it up.

If the attacks are becoming regular or sustained, it's time to take action. It's highly unlikely it will stop of its own accord. If you don't do anything, it's giving the person unwritten permission to continue, which isn't good for either of you.

You need to explain to them how their anger is affecting you: what it feels like at the time, how you feel afterwards, and the damage it is doing to your relationship. Of course, this may invite further attack. They turn it around and blame you in some way, even accuse you of being the one at fault. If this happens each time you raise the issue, it is time to seriously question the relationship.

Some occasions are better than others for this kind of conversation. The heat of the moment is definitely a no-no. It needs to be when you are both calm. It may help to put it in writing first, especially if you are afraid of hurting them or what their reaction might be. It can be a softer approach, giving them a chance to absorb your thoughts and to respond in a similar way if they wish.

It helps to think about boundaries beforehand. Perhaps talk it over with someone neutral. Is it zero tolerance from now on or are you prepared to accept a certain level of behaviour? What are the consequences if things continue the way they are? Are you willing to work through it with them or will that be the end?

The best outcome is that they take on board what you are saying, acknowledge their behaviour, and do something about it. But with the best will in the world, this won't always happen or only in part. There are promises to change, but then the same old behaviour and excuses start creeping back in. They need to understand this is about committing to change in the long term. A sticking plaster apology isn't enough.

Ultimately, if someone can't control their anger, it's their problem. Sometimes the best thing to do is walk away from the wreckage.

anger as a catalyst of change

Some people see anger as a completely negative force that serves no purpose. But if we're open to listening, it can be a great source of information about our inner selves. It lets us know something is wrong. Working out what this is puts the power in our hands. We don't have to be a victim of circumstance.

We see this in a wider way. Anger has been a driver of social change, bringing people together to fight for fairness and equality. The trick is harnessing the anger; channelling it into what will make the most difference.

Social change doesn't happen overnight and it's the same when we're making changes in our lives. Our anger might demand instant results, wanting its own way now, not tomorrow, but it needs the thinking brain to see the bigger picture and work out strategies. This can be tiring for the mind, and we might become weary and discouraged. That's when it's time to restoke the fire in the belly. Used positively, anger can be the fuel that drives us forward.

7 the path of the spiritual warrior

The idea of the spiritual warrior is a stirring one. If only we could be like that, we think. Well, we can. Everyday life is the perfect arena for nurturing the warrior within us.

the irrepressible spirit

No matter how much we meditate, light candles, and put Buddha figures around the house, it isn't enough for some of us. Not that we don't appreciate short periods of quiet and calm, but it's difficult to sustain. We become fidgety and restless, even agitated.

In our attempts to be tranquil, we may start suppressing our natural liveliness. We convince ourselves it's working for a time, adopting an air that says, I am serene, all is well with my world. But it's like forcing a tent into a tiny drawstring bag. We shove a portion of it in only for another part to billow out.

This is where the spiritual warrior comes in. It's an alternative for those of us who need something more energetic and outward looking.

the warrior way

For psychologist Carl Jung, The Warrior is one of the twelve main archetypes. These mythical characters are universal to us all, residing deep in our collective psyche.

The figure appears in many spiritual practices and faiths. There are the Christian Knights of the Round Table on the quest for the Holy Grail; Vajrapani, the Buddhist Bodhisattva, wielding a diamond thunderbolt; and Krishna, the Hindu God, on the battlefield in The Mahabharata.

The Warrior has bold symbolism, appearing in yoga as a powerful posture with front knee bent, back leg on a diagonal, arms outstretched and eyes ahead. Astrology has Sagittarius; half-human half-horse, poised with bow and arrow.

Spiritual warriors face and overcome fear. They understand that self-doubt and lack of confidence get in the way of spiritual development. We release our power and potential by tuning into the energy within ourselves, not repressing it.

Unlike the contemplative life of the monk or hermit, the spiritual warrior is out in the world, doing what they can for the good of humankind, even if this means going against the grain. They won't take the easy option or let themselves off the hook. They understand the essential truth of existence – we live in houses of sand. Better to face this with courage than live in an illusion of safety.

taking heart

We tend to pigeonhole courage to heroic acts, like saving a life or battles with adversity. Moved and humbled, we put the individuals on a pedestal, seeing bravery as something for a select few. But we can all be courageous. It's just a case of cultivating it.

It doesn't mean never being scared. It's feeling the fear but doing it anyway. This may have become a self-help cliché but it stands true. Few of us are truly fearless. Think about athletes and performers. Many of them experience nerves or anxiety, whether it's sweating palms or nagging self-doubt. The trick is not to let it become so overwhelming that it paralyses us. Fear is normal. At a very basic level it's our biology, the flight, fight or freeze response. Acknowledging it can lessen its power.

Bravery is a relative concept. While some people love speaking in front of an audience, it's terrifying for others. What matters is your own measure; working out your individual yardstick then starting small. Courage is often best built little by little. Going too far out of your comfort zone can be intimidating, making you scuttle back to your place of safety.

Pat yourself on the back regularly. It helps to boost your confidence, as does looking back to see how far you've come. If you trip up along the way, remind yourself that it happens, you're only human. Going back and trying again develops your resilience and resolve.

Courage is one of the bests gifts to ourselves. As it grows, we feel less limited and intimidated by life. The fear never goes away, but it can become a spur.

navigating the rocky road

The path of the spiritual warrior isn't an easy one. It means standing up and being counted, and this puts us in the firing line.

People won't always respond well or in ways we expect. Whether it's disapproval, ridicule or jealousy, we will be on the receiving end at some point or other. It goes with the territory. This is why it's important to build up our inner resources, so we have a strong foundation to work from.

It doesn't mean getting things right all the time. We all make mistakes. But it's being prepared to face our shortcomings and address them. If we're speaking out or setting an example, we have to be willing to scrutinise our motives and actions. Are we being rebellious for the sake of it or getting too pumped up with righteous indignation or self-importance?

We also have to check the tendency to be over-zealous. Sometimes a lightness of touch is needed to win people to our side.

tapping into your inner hero

Visualisation is a way of having ready access to your inner hero. In this technique, you create a character in your mind's eye that can be called upon when needed.

It's important that the character is based on you, not a being outside of yourself. This may seem odd, that you're the superhero or god, but that's the point – we all have a spiritual warrior within us.

You can be whoever you like. You might choose a Celt, Samurai, or one of the Buddhist Bodhisattvas. Are you human, godly or a mixture of both? Do you have a gender and age? Maybe you're drawn to an animal or favourite fantasy figure.

What is your character's status? Are you royalty, warrior, healer or artist? Perhaps you come from the natural world and are part river or tree.

If you have clothes, what are you wearing? Think about the colours and textures. Perhaps you have unusual coloured skin or are covered in tattoos.

Do you have a particular stance or pose, like the classic archer or sitting Buddha? If your character moves, do you stride, gallop, fly or float?

What is the setting? It could be a forest, mountain or underwater land. Is there anything that stands out for you when you look around? Is the scene still or moving? Are there other characters or creatures?

When it comes to your character's qualities, think about the traits you value, such as kindness, fearlessness or humour. How does your character demonstrate these? Also consider what you use for protection. Do you wield a shining sword or thunderbolt? Perhaps you wear charms or a glowing cloak.

Once you have developed your character, focusing on their qualities can give you support. If you have a tough day ahead, draw on their determination and strength. If you feel vulnerable, call to mind their means of protection.

Visit them in their setting to help you work through problems or for empathy and comfort. You are talking to yourself, of course, but it is a higher or better part of you, giving an alternative or wider perspective.

There is nothing stopping you inventing other characters. These might be completely separate or complement the original. They can have conversations with each other or come together in imaginative scenarios. Have a play and see what unfolds.

daring to shine

We often hold ourselves back through fear of what others think. We don't want to seem too full of ourselves or over-confident. We might be afraid of being made fun of or making others feel inadequate.

Part of being a spiritual warrior is letting your light shine. As writer and spiritual teacher Marianne Williamson says: 'Our deepest fear is not that we are inadequate. Our deepest fear is that we are powerful beyond measure. It is our light, not our darkness that most frightens us. We ask ourselves, 'Who am I to be brilliant, gorgeous, talented, fabulous?' Actually, who are you not to be?'.

When we give ourselves permission to shine, we become a light in the world. There will always be people who want to dim our shine, but it says more about them than us. If we don't take the risk, how can we inspire others to do the same? In the words of Brene Brown, author of 'Daring Greatly': 'Courage starts with showing up and letting ourselves be seen.' Dare to live wide.

8 spreading kindness

Kindness is one of the cornerstones of a life well lived. It doesn't need a faith or any special equipment. We can all 'do' kindness anywhere and at any time. But it has its pitfalls. Spreading kindness isn't as simple as throwing out fairy dust. While it can work its magic, sometimes it blows back in our faces.

starting with self-compassion

Kindness starts with the self, but this can be hard to get our heads around. While we wouldn't think twice about showing kindness to a stranger in the street, it feels indulgent when it comes to ourselves. But as the saying goes, you can't pour from an empty cup. We all need replenishing. Self-compassion does this, helping to maintain our inner being.

Take the carer or parent who gives and gives without showing themselves care. This can be draining, leading to emotional exhaustion and ill health. It may create resentment, taking the person down the road of martyrdom. None of this helps what might already be a difficult situation.

If you have poor mental health, self-compassion is vital. Without it, self-dislike and loathing have room to play. This can make life hard – not only for you but for the loved ones around you struggling to help. Being kind to yourself is a way of being kind to others.

The good news is, we can all develop self-compassion.

The first step is challenging your thinking. Do you encourage others to be self-compassionate but don't practice it yourself? This is lop-sided. What makes you so undeserving compared to everyone else? After all, there isn't a cap on kindness. There's plenty to go around.

Unfortunately, it isn't easy to turn off the critical voice in our heads once it gets going. Try gently quietening it instead. Ask it to lower the volume or give you a break for a period of time.

Sidestep your internal critic by thinking what you would you say to a friend, partner or family member. A rotten day has left you feeling tired and upset. How might you support and encourage a loved one in that situation?

Write yourself permission slips. These work best when they're specific and time-limited, such as, 'I give myself permission to switch off from my problems this evening'. This technique can help cultivate your ability to rest and recuperate. Mind, spirit and body need time to relax and recover, especially in difficult periods. Healing can't happen without it.

Build up a stock of items that foster self-compassion. This might be songs, poems, objects or inspirational pieces of writing. Write a letter to yourself or ask friends and family to send you letters. These can be read when you need reminding or for comfort.

Some people find meditation helpful, particularly The Metta Bhavana, or Loving Kindness meditation. This is a compassion practice in five stages, starting with the self and opening out to all beings. It can seem at first odd, focusing on yourself, but it's where kindness begins.

creating ripples

Being kind to others makes us feel good about ourselves. It produces endorphins in the brain, giving us the 'helper's high'. This also happens when we see others being kind. Social Psychologist Jonathan Haidt calls it 'elevation'. It inspires us to be better people and helps to undo the unpleasant feelings created by bad news stories.

Random acts of kindness are a way of spreading good feeling in the world. They don't have to be big or take much time. If you're in a supermarket queue and the person behind you is in a hurry, letting them go before you might reduce some of their stress and get them to where they need to be sooner. This could have a knock-on effect on their day and the people they come into contact with. In this way, our actions ripple out.

The Random Acts of Kindness Foundation believes that if millions of us do our bit like this, it creates a powerful global synergy. By helping others, we are ultimately helping ourselves.

being real not ideal

Living a life led by kindness has a strong appeal. But it's a big ask. If being kind all the time is the bar, anything less can be felt as a failure. It's one of the quickest ways to come up against our shortcomings.

Thinking of kindness as a practice rather than a way of being keeps it real. We're just practising; we don't have to be perfect. This less rigid approach allows for lapses – which we all have.

It means you don't always have to feel kind to be kind. A friend asks for help at short notice or a family problem disrupts your plans. Reluctance or irritation in these situations is natural. What matters is what you do, not what you think.

Part of the practice is developing the ability to receive kindness as well as give it. We have to watch we're not putting ourselves on an odd kind of moral high ground; we are the giver, others are there to receive from us. Kindness isn't a one-sided coin. It can develop into largesse if we're not careful, being over-liberal with our time, care or money. This is about making ourselves feel good. We're so caught up in our own generosity, we don't notice how uncomfortable or patronised we may be making people feel.

Kindness isn't all. It can be overdone. Instead of encouraging a person to do things for themselves, we do too much for them, not allowing them to build their capacity or confidence. This can slip into controlling behaviour or create dependency.

Another pitfall is forgetting kindness closer to home. The classic example is a person with missionary zeal to do good in the world while neglecting their loved ones. In many respects, it's easier to show kindness to people we don't know, but kindness isn't just for strangers. We forget to make the same effort with our family and friends, squabbling over something trivial or not listening when they're talking to us. It's not that we're being unintentionally unkind, but sometimes we leave our care at the front door.

when kindness blows back

It's joyful to send kindness out into the world. There it goes, like fairy dust, spreading the magic. We hope, of course, that it will come back to us at some point in the future. Doesn't kindness always lead to more kindness? Unfortunately, not. This is a rose-tinted view. In reality, it sometimes hits a wall or even blows back in our faces.

Not everyone on the receiving end of kindness is inspired to it themselves. Some people are happy to let the giver keep giving. We've all heard the saying, making a rod for your own back. This is a road that many a kind person has gone down. The danger is it wears us out or we start to feel resentment.

Sometimes the person on the receiving end of our care turns on us. We may have become someone to vent their frustration and anger on. But being kind, we give them the benefit of the doubt. This can make them turn on us all the more.

Being kind doesn't give us a glowing, protective force field. If anything, it can make us more vulnerable. Sometimes we have to hold back on the kindness. This may go against the grain, but it's important to look after ourselves - which takes us back to self-compassion.

9 letting go of letting go

Letting go is a common spiritual theme. We're encouraged to loosen our hold on yesterday's troubles and make peace with the past. But it isn't always that simple. Letting go can be challenging, and our failure to do so may make us cling on all the more.

it's human to hang on

It's painful to let go. It means saying goodbye or admitting defeat. We lose a loved one, our security or health. Life isn't what it was. We can't stop dwelling on what it was like before, as if there was some way of bringing it back just by thinking about it.

This is normal behaviour, but if we cling too hard and long it becomes unhealthy. We become the proverbial dog with a bone, caught up in powerful negative states like anger and bitterness. Ultimately, we need to loosen the grip, if not let go altogether.

a gradual loosening

'Let it go' people say, as if we could wave a wand and our problems vanish in an instant. But if it were that simple, we would do it.

When we can't let go, it's often because we're not yet at a place where we can. The longer it has gone on, the more difficult it can be – and trying to get rid of it can make it stick harder than ever.

We sometimes trick ourselves, of course. We think we've let go, which gives us a temporary sense of relief, but back it comes as fierce as ever. We've now added a sense of failure to the pot.

While the idea of completely letting go is an attractive one, it's too big a leap for many of us. A more realistic and kinder approach is to see it as a process; something to be done in stages rather than all at once.

When people tell us it's time to let go, it's usually because they have unwritten time limits they are judging us by. A more organic approach understands that we usually have to work our way through issues, and this can take months or even years.

Sometimes we never completely let go but find the problem doesn't fill our lives as much. Time often does this work, allowing us to become more distanced. In this way, rather than trying to set our burden down too early, the load gradually lightens. We might even wake up one morning and realise we are not carrying it any more.

This said, there are circumstances where hanging on is the right thing to do. Perhaps we're fighting for justice or trying to make something work. Letting go can be seen as giving up, and it might not be the time to surrender just yet.

keeping forgiveness real

Forgiveness often raises its head when it comes to letting go. Jack Kornfield, one of the leading Buddhist practitioners in America, describes it as 'the capacity to let go, to release the suffering, the sorrows, the burdens of the pains and betrayals of the past, and instead to choose the mystery of love'. By hanging on to bitter feelings we hurt ourselves most. Forgiveness replaces this hurt with healing.

But it isn't always that straightforward. Trying to be the better person can put us under unnecessary emotional pressure. We hear stories of parents forgiving their child's murderer or torture victims making peace with their captors. If they can do it, why can't we? It makes us feel uncaring, even bad people. It also means we might deny ourselves the natural expression of anger and hurt, seeing it as wrong rather than understandable in the circumstances.

Like letting go, forgiveness may be better approached as a process rather than an act. It isn't about one side declaiming 'I forgive you!' while the other kneels before them. It's having a dialogue in which both parties work towards resolution. This usually takes time and a willingness to have difficult conversations.

When we're intent on the act of forgiveness, we may avoid challenging unacceptable behaviour. Take a person who is being abused by a partner. If the abuser hears they are forgiven without having to change the way they behave, it's a green light to continue.

Spiritual writings tend to take the view that we can't heal or move on without forgiving people. But it isn't always necessary and may slow recovery down, especially if the person doesn't show any remorse. It's more honest to acknowledge that while we would like to forgive, sometimes we can't. As the saying goes, To err is human, to forgive divine. We're not divine.

the art of allowing

Acceptance is a major theme in spirituality and one that we can struggle with. When life throws balls of thorny bramble our way, our automatic reaction is to knock them back, not pick them up and embrace them.

Like letting go, spiritual and self-help books can be very black and white about acceptance. Acceptance is good, non-acceptance is bad. It's one or the other with no middle ground.

A gentler approach is to allow rather than to accept. It creates space where we can park difficulties. We may not be happy with them but we don't have to force ourselves to accept them or let them go. We can just let them be.

10 everyday blessings

Being thankful is good for us. It boosts our immune system, lowers our blood pressure and makes us happier. Yet it's all too easy to let thankfulness sit in the corner of our lives. This chapter dusts it down and takes a fresh look.

the balm to life's uncertainty

We live with the possibility of loss every day. Whether it's our belongings, health or loved ones, we can lose it all in an instant. No wonder we put our energies into maintaining what we have – and trying to get more of it. It's an attempt to bolster ourselves against the world. But it can lead to a mindset that focuses on lack. If only the sun was brighter, if only we had more money, love, energy, time. Thankfulness gets pushed into the background.

Robert Emmons, Professor of Psychology at the University of California, has spent over a decade studying gratitude. In his view, not only does a grateful attitude help, it is essential, especially in tough times. It acts as a kind of psychological immune system: 'In the face of demoralization, gratitude has the power to energize. In the face of brokenness, gratitude has the power to heal. In the face of despair, gratitude has the power to bring hope.' Thankfulness is the balm to our uncertain world.

tuning in to opportunities

One way of becoming more thankful is to widen the scope of what gives us appreciative feelings. There are possibilities all around, it's just a matter of tuning into them.

The trick is to be specific, not generalise. People often say they are thankful for their good health, but it can be broken down into multiple reasons. Our levels of health mean we can get out into the countryside for a walk, travel to meet up with friends or enjoy a good meal. Using this approach, someone dealing with illness can still find things to be thankful for.

Managing to get out of bed to sit in the garden might be seen as a gift.

Take time each day to be mindful of small, everyday blessings. Keeping a gratitude diary is one way of doing this and has proven effective for people with depression and long-term health conditions. Some people write on scraps of paper, put them in a jar and watch them build up over the year.

Another technique is to reflect on our interconnectedness. Our food, clothes and belongings don't appear out of thin air. Numerous connections lead to it all being there. As such, we all owe a debt of gratitude to others and to the planet. This is thankfulness in the bigger picture, and we can all share in it.

saying thank you and meaning it

Good manners help us navigate life in a smoother way, but we often fall into the habit of saying a polite thank you without meaning it.

Part of cultivating thankfulness is developing our ability to express it to others. Sometimes social awkwardness stops us, but the more we do it the easier it becomes.

It doesn't have to be face to face. You could write a note, email, or leave a small token, like flowers. Whether it's a waiter, teacher, neighbour or work colleague, everyone gets a boost from a nice thank you - and giving one makes us feel good too.

appreciating the best

When we're self-critical, we focus on our faults and how to fix them. This is where Appreciative Inquiry can help.

Appreciative Inquiry is a social constructionist model developed in the 1990s. It encourages us to think about what we are doing well, our positive qualities and what is going right in our lives.

If we were unhappy and using traditional problem-solving, we might ask what was making us miserable and how we could change it. With Appreciative Enquiry, we look at what makes us happy and our ideas and hopes around increasing our enjoyment of life. It's more than an exercise in looking for the positives. It helps to free up thinking, so we are more open to possibility and potential.

As an approach, it stresses the importance of the words we use to create our world. What we say and the stories we tell each other becomes our version of the truth. If a couple continually talk about the problems between them, this constructs a shared reality of a relationship that isn't doing well. Instead, they could look at what they appreciate in the relationship and each other, using it as a base to share their hopes about what might work well in the future. This builds on the best rather than the worst.

waste not want not

One way of practising thankfulness is to recycle and re-use wherever we can. We forget how recent the convenience culture is. Not so many years ago, people stored brown paper in a drawer, made the Sunday joint last into the week and repaired clothes rather than throwing them away.

How often do we run the tap without thinking how lucky we are to have clean water? We're so careless with something that would be a lifeline for others. Whether it's only buying the food we need, re-using plastic bags or drying clothes on the line instead of the washing machine, there are ways of showing more appreciation of our resources. It's also better for the planet!

adjusting the yardstick

Millions of people all over the world don't have the basics – shelter, warmth and food – but how many of us use this yardstick? We tend to compare ourselves to those with more than us, whatever that 'more' may be: more money, a bigger house, better social life. This creates a default position of want with its constant niggle of dissatisfaction.

If poverty becomes our measure, we immediately become rich. Instead of craving what we don't have, we become thankful for what we do have. But to get to this, we have to open our eyes to the world.

When we watch the news and see people in dire situations like war and famine, it's easy to switch off. Not just clicking the remote control but switching off mentally. Disassociating can be a way of coping with how brutal life can be. When our parents used to say 'Children are starving in Africa!' at the dinner table, how many of us really understood what that meant? We'd feel a little guilty but still not eat all our greens the next time.

To truly shift the yardstick, we need to take a few moments at least to reflect, allowing ourselves to connect with the experience of other people.

This isn't just about far off countries. Poverty is on our doorstep. It may be more comfortable to think that people only have themselves to blame – their lifestyle, poor choices or laziness – but most of us are only a few degrees away from hardship. Disability and illness, unemployment, bereavement – all of these things can quickly put us in a state of need.

We don't need to throw off all our worldly goods, it's just about acknowledging how much we have compared to others. We can show this by donating to causes, taking used goods to the charity shop or volunteering our time. We can also speak up for people in need. This might be signing petitions or challenging negative views on social media.

Is your glass half full or half empty? The choice is yours.

sometimes thankfulness comes later

People say there's something to be thankful for in every situation. While there may be truth in this, it isn't always easy to see at the time.

Take a parent with a critically ill child in hospital. They tell themselves they should be thankful for the care their child is receiving, but it feels impossible in the circumstances. This makes them feel ungrateful, adding to their distress.

A cancer patient has been told they will get better. They try to feel thankful – there are so many others with a different diagnosis – but the chemotherapy is tough and the illness is having a negative impact on their life.

It's hard to feel grateful in the middle of challenging situations. Trying to force it on ourselves isn't self-compassionate.

It's the same with difficult people in our lives. There is the idea that everyone has something to teach us, but we don't always see the lessons straight away.

Robert Emmons talks about remembering the bad, looking back to make a comparison with where we are now. Time lends distance. This is how we might reach the point where we can see positives in having gone through the worst. Sometimes thankfulness comes later.

11 re-thinking the brain

Our brains are incredible pieces of biological hardware. Finger-like dendrites branch out from more than a hundred billion brain cells, creating around ten trillion possible connections for electrical messages to whizz along.

These connections aren't set in stone. The beauty of the brain is its neuronal plasticity. Unlike machines, we're designed to constantly change and evolve. This means we can literally change our minds.

changing our minds

The pathways in the brain aren't fixed but we do have habitual thought patterns. Anyone dogged by repetitive anxious or depressed thoughts knows how stubborn they can be. If they seem to be so much a part of us, it's because they are. Their neural tracks are a physical reality in our brains. Those particular neurons are switched on while others lie dormant.

The good news is, we can reconfigure our brains. The strength of neural connections depends on how much they are used. The trick is changing the data we put into the brain and reinforcing it to create new pathways. By changing our thoughts, we can change our brain.

There are a range of techniques and programmes to help us do this, Cognitive Behavioural Therapy (CBT) being the most well-known. It teaches us how to identify unhelpful thought patterns, called Automatic Thoughts. This might be magnifying the negative and minimising the positive – doing badly in a test proves how stupid we are but doing well is luck – or catastrophising about how things will turn out.

Automatic Thoughts are often based on emotional reasoning. We feel something to be true, so it must be true. This way, a high achiever sees themselves as a failure or a popular person thinks they are unloved. We address the thoughts by collecting evidence to challenge them. This generates more balanced thinking, based in reality rather than our imaginations.

A popular mind management programme is The Chimp Paradox by Dr Steve Peters, the man who contributed to Britain's amazing success in the 2012 Olympics. He separates the mind into three areas: the Chimp, our emotional and impulsive self; the Human, our rational self; and the Superego or Computer that governs memory and automatic behaviour. The programme shows us how to train the Chimp so we become happier, more confident and healthier.

There are obvious advantages to following tried and tested programmes, but they don't suit everyone. CBT can take a while to get to grips with and may feel like a sticking plaster over your problems. Sometimes it's a case of drawing from different models to use what works with you and your brain.

transforming over time

Some people have life-changing experiences leading to an immediate mental shift. But it isn't a quick fix for most of us; transformation takes time. We have years of conditioning and life experience behind us, shaping who we are and how we think. We're not automatons, to be reconfigured in one afternoon.

We're often unrealistic about how long change is going to take. We hope we'll be a good way along, if not done, by the time we finish a course or a book. But we often only understand in a theoretical way. We have to test it out and reflect on it in the light of experience. It might be a year or two after doing a programme like CBT that we only start to get it. Being fatigued, ill or emotionally raw slows us further. Negative thoughts are very resistant, and it's exhausting to keep challenging them. We may need to show ourselves compassion and step back from mind management for a time.

Sometimes our circumstances give us good reason for the round of negative thoughts. Someone who has lost their job at the same time as being diagnosed with a serious illness can be forgiven for thinking life is tough. We can't always mentally turn things around for ourselves – at least not immediately.

We have to trust that our brain is doing its work. We might not be aware of it, but that doesn't mean it isn't happening. It's often only down the road that we see, and feel, the change.

watching the flow

We can think of our thoughts as a river. Sometimes we're caught up in the middle, being carried to where we don't want to be, but with practice we can pull ourselves out and sit on the riverbank. Not only can we watch the flow from there, we're able to consciously slow it down.

Mindfulness and meditation are key ways of building the skills to do this. It takes practice and mental discipline, but we can all develop our minds this way.

Learning to observe our thoughts shows us that we don't have to take them so seriously. We notice our regular visitors, like Automatic Thoughts, and understand they are just mental happenings. Something triggers them and off they go, triggering other thoughts in turn like a line of falling dominoes.

We don't have to let them take us down their well-worn tracks, just let them play out like old scratchy records before they fade.

being in two minds

Being pulled in different directions by competing thoughts can be uncomfortable. But the ability to be in two, or more, minds at once can open up our thinking. It's mentally healthy to consider alternative views; a sign of a broader mind, not one stuck in rigid ways of thinking about the world.

We don't always have to take a definite position. Our brains are more than capable of carrying several tracks of thought at the same time. This allows us to embrace the ambiguity of human experience. There are multiple thoughts to choose from, diverse ways of seeing things. Why pin ourselves down if we don't have to?

There are times, of course, when we have to make choices. But ambivalence encourages us to think matters through rather than making snap decisions. This isn't indecisiveness; it only becomes that if we continue to waver.

Ultimately, there is usually some anxiety and regret whichever way we go on a difficult decision. We can only make what seems to be the best choice at the time.

keeping the brain in shape

We are all creatures of habit, even the most free-spirited person. We have our little routines and ways of doing things. The risk is that we become prisoners of processes. 'We've always done it this way' becomes the mantra to resist change rather than embrace it.

This inhibits creative thinking. Ground-breaking developments in science, technology and the arts come from looking at things in a new way.

Our routines don't have to be set in stone. Making changes is good for the brain and keeps us primed for unexpected events. We never know what's around the corner. Change is part of life and being adaptable is a key life skill.

Stack your washing up a different way, sleep on the other side of the bed, alter your route to work or use your toothbrush with the opposite hand. Activities like this challenge the brain, helping to keep neural connections strong. As the saying goes, use it or lose it. This is especially important as we age and the brain's plasticity declines.

Puzzles, games and lifelong learning all help to keep the brain young. Mentally active people have less beta-amyloid protein, the sticky plaque that is a hallmark of Alzheimer's. A fitter brain is also more resilient, so the impact of an illness like dementia takes longer.

It also helps us keep a sense of potential and possibility as we age. For some older people, it's as if their thinking has gone along the same well-worn tracks so many times, their view of the world becomes narrower and narrower. How much better to open to wisdom.

12 quietening the mind

Meditation is an antidote to the stresses and speed of modern life. It's a low-cost activity that's easy to introduce into our lives. But the meditation journey has pitfalls as well as plusses. Instead of quietening the mind, we might agitate it.

the monkey mind

We have an estimated seventy thousand thoughts a day. Whatever the actual number, we only have to observe our thinking for a few moments to be aware of the constant play of thoughts. Given that we have more than a hundred billion brain cells, with trillions of possible connections, the Monkey Mind has a huge playground to leap around in.

Research suggests that many of our thoughts are the same as the day before. It's just mental junk going around in a loop. Negative thoughts particularly replay over and over, leading us into increasingly depressed or worried states.

Meditation is a way of stilling these thoughts and creating mental calm. It's good for the body too, reducing the effects of stress and helping to regulate our day-night cycles.

The question is, where to start?

an ageless art

There isn't one way to 'do' meditation. While Buddhist traditions are the most well-known, numerous practices have developed over time. Their shared feature is deliberate attention of the mind. Meditation isn't going into a trance; it's a very conscious activity.

While there can be movement, as in yoga, the meditator usually sits still. Beginners are often keen on the classic Lotus posture, but this can be physically challenging. Most people sit in a simpler cross-legged position, kneel astride cushions or use a chair. It's finding a posture that prevents slumping while being comfortable to maintain. There may be some initial discomfort but it shouldn't be persistently painful.

In its simplest form, meditators give attention to the breath as it moves in and out of the body. This might be noticing the inhalation and exhalation through the nostrils or widening attention to the rise and fall of the lungs. The breath can also be counted or manipulated.

Some meditators just sit with whatever arises in the body or mind, while others use techniques like visualisation to cultivate kindness and compassion. There can be a point of focus: repeated words or sounds, such as the 'Om' mantra or a prayer, or crystals, candles and other objects with a spiritual meaning.

Whatever the method, the Monkey Mind wanders off, day dreaming, planning and worrying. The idea is to notice and gently bring the attention back. This can happen numerous times during a meditation, especially for beginners. It's part of the discipline and why it can be helpful to practice under the guidance of a teacher.

Most schools encourage practice at least once or twice a day. This can be up to an hour or more, but five or ten minutes is often enough. The aim is to make meditation part of everyday routine, like brushing the teeth.

a moment on mindfulness

In many respects, mindfulness is the same as meditation, and the terms are often used interchangeably. However, meditation tends to refer to formal sitting practice whereas mindfulness has a wider use.

Through mindfulness, we bring our attention to the present moment, experiencing it as it is without trying to fix or change anything. It encourages us to be more aware of our internal and external worlds, to notice things we hadn't seen before – or had stopped noticing.

We can practise mindfulness anywhere and at any time, even during the most everyday of activities. It's a way of approaching life afresh. We may have done something many times before but it is always new in the moment.

If we were eating an apple mindfully, we would give it our full attention, even before taking a bite. We might feel its surface, holding it to our nose to take in its smell. As we ate it, we would be aware of how it felt in the mouth, noting the sensations as we swallowed it down. Even when we finished, we might be aware of how the core felt against our fingers and listen for the sound as it landed in the recycle bin.

In recent years, mindfulness has been brought together with Cognitive Behavioural Therapy (CBT) and proven to improve mental wellbeing. In their book 'The Mindful Way through Depression', Mark Williams, John Teasdale, Zindel Segal and Jon Kabat-Zinn explore how the practice encourages us step back from the never-ending commentary of negative thoughts. We learn they are just mental events, a product of our thinking habits and not necessarily the truth. We don't have to attach to them so much.

Few of us are brought up with a mindful approach to life, but it's a practice we can all learn to take more enjoyment in the world around us.

setting off on the road

The internet is a good place to start. There are numerous websites with audio and video clips, many for free, so there's no need to pay a subscription or buy products at this stage. Do some searching and see what naturally draws you. We often need to try out different practices to find what suits us.

Your local library will probably have books you can borrow or there's a wide selection online and in bookshops. A beginner's guide can be useful, especially with guided meditations on a CD or DVD.

It can be helpful to go on a meditation course or taster. Despite the growing use of mindfulness in mental health services, most group opportunities tend to be spiritual rather than secular. However, it's possible to participate in group meditation without taking on a religion or particular set of beliefs. It depends on who is offering it and how important it is to them that people identify with their community.

Bear in mind that you may find some approaches too religious or culturally challenging. Try not to take this as a failure on your part. One way isn't superior to another.

While meditation can be practised anywhere, the setting is usually an indoor room in a place of worship, community venue or holistic business. It helps if the space is private and quiet as it can be difficult to sit with noise and distraction, especially when new to it.

The practice is usually led by a leader or teacher. They will have had, and probably still have, teachers themselves. They're likely to give some kind of introduction, telling you something about themselves, their organisation and practice. It helps if they give you an idea how long the meditation is going to last – usually around ten to fifteen minutes for beginners – and if there is a signal to mark the beginning and end, such as the ringing of a bell. It can be unsettling if they plunge straight in.

There might be a chance to try out different sitting postures before the meditation begins. You probably won't hit on the right one straight away, but you can always play around with cushions at home afterwards. It's more important to be comfortable, otherwise it can be a distraction.

There should always be a couple of seats available for those who need them. You should never feel pressured into going on the floor.

During the meditation, your thoughts will probably wander. The Monkey Mind runs around taking it all in. You're curious about a noise outside, your back aches, you wonder what to have for dinner. This is normal.

It's also normal to feel the same at the end of the practice as you did at the beginning. Few are filled with tranquil bliss, especially the first time.

After the meditation, there may be refreshments and a chance to chat. Some people can be keen to tell you how amazing it was; they felt like they were flying or it reminded them of an awesome meditation they had in an Indian ashram. Try not to let it take from your experience. Everyone's journey is different, and some people may be trying to impress.

Regular doses of group meditation can support and motivate you in your individual practice. It can take some getting used to – you might feel self-consciousness at first or out of your comfort zone – but once you settle in, it has a different quality to meditating alone.

There are less opportunities for moving meditation, but it makes sense to start with sitting practice. You can learn the basic skills, which can then be applied to movement.

Yoga is a great complement to sitting practice, particularly in developing mindfulness. Teachers vary in their approach though – some have a more mindful approach than others - so it's finding the right person for you.

off the beaten track

Going on a meditation retreat is a chance to step back from daily life. It offers time for reflection and self-development, usually from a spiritual or holistic angle. Most centres are in the countryside and have programmes catering for the beginner up to the seasoned meditator.

Introductory retreats are geared to beginners. They're usually for a weekend up to a week and are an opportunity to experience guided meditation and learn about Buddhism or other perspectives. If you like to be active or outdoors, you may be better suited to a yoga, walking or photography retreat.

Be aware that centres can be quite regimented. They usually have set times for meditation and meals, and the days start early. Most have expectations around behaviour, such as not drinking alcohol or limiting use of mobile phones.

The communal experience can be challenging if you like regular time on your own. Some centres have single bedrooms, but in most you have to share with at least one person. It can make you acutely aware of how intolerant you can sometimes be. Going on retreat rarely transforms us into shiny happy beings who get on well with everyone. The opposite can happen, especially if it's a crowded centre or everyone is stuck indoors due to poor weather.

Many of us go on retreat at difficult times in our lives but this doesn't mean we'll find the ease and peace we are looking for. Instead of leaving our troubles at the door, we often carry them in. The retreat may bring up difficult emotions or face us with challenging aspects of ourselves.

Before you go, it is worth thinking about how you might look after yourself. While your aim might be to get through the retreat without contact with loved ones, some emotional support might be helpful. A phone call or two could make all the difference to the experience, so keep it in mind as a possibility.

Don't feel you have to dive in, sharing your life story with strangers on the first night. It's up to you how much personal information you disclose. Sometimes we get swept along and share things that we later wish we had kept private.

You don't have to take part in all the structured activity if you don't want to. Have some time to yourself if you need it. Getting involved in practical tasks, like gardening and housework, can help to keep you grounded and centre staff always appreciate the help.

Try to go outdoors regularly, whether it's the centre grounds or further afield. This gives you some space and helps with cabin fever. If you need a dose of normality, take a break off site and go to a local town or village. If it's some distance away and you don't have a car, see if you can join centre staff driving out for supplies.

Be prepared for at least one period of silence. While few retreats are fully silent, there may be a taster for an afternoon or evening. It can feel strange at first and generate amusement as people work out how to communicate without talking, but there can be something quite special about a group of people sharing silence together. It can also be oddly emotional, so don't be surprised if feelings come up.

Try not to compare yourself to others or get involved in competition. Let people get on with sitting in the Lotus pose though it gives them back ache and seeing who can meditate the longest.

Retreats don't have to be an endurance test to make them worthwhile. Be aware that some are completely silent with hours of sitting meditation and fasting each day. They are not for everyone. You can still develop spiritually and in a profound way without putting yourself through that kind of experience.

If you're really not enjoying the retreat and it's affecting your wellbeing, you can always leave early. This doesn't mean you would feel like that every time. It may be something about your current circumstances or the nature of that retreat. They can be demanding, especially if your mental health is at a low ebb – you're dealing with depression or a bereavement, say. Sometimes it's better to wait until you feel more resilient.

going it alone

Some centres offer solitary retreats, a period of time to live like a hermit in a meditation hut or similar. This can be an intense experience and isn't recommended for the beginner. It's too much for some seasoned meditators.

An alternative is to try a solitary retreat at home.

It's advisable to start small, a half day or day at the most. You'll get more from a few quality hours than stretching it out for the sake of it.

It helps to structure the time in advance; set your meditation and meal times, with mindful activity in between. This could be reading, yoga or a task, like cleaning out a cupboard. Plan your meals, ideally healthy vegetarian, so you can have your shopping in ready and cook from scratch. Switch off phones, the computer and TV, and aim to rise early.

Solitary retreats can bring up lonely or difficult feelings. Sometimes we work through them and they pass, but there is always the option of cutting the retreat short. Ultimately, it should be a nourishing rather than punishing experience.

steps rather than strides

Meditation promises to make us calmer, happier and healthier, but it's usually a slow burn rather than a quick fix. The changes can be so subtle, it may be some time down the line before we feel the benefits.

Daily practice can become dull, the mental equivalent of doing an exercise regime each day. We may wonder if it's worth labouring on, especially if we don't seem to be getting much out of it.

We may hear people talk about exciting meditative experiences, known as Kundalini. They're filled with light or feel waves of energy rushing through them. Kundalini aren't essential to the meditative experience, and are often seen as a distraction, but we may feel we are missing out.

If nothing else, we might expect to have more inner peace, but even this can be evasive, especially if we're depressed, anxious or unwell. It can be harder to concentrate and more tiring to keep pulling the mind back. Negative thoughts and feelings can come up, quite powerfully at times. The longer we sit, the worse we feel.

In these circumstances, it's better to keep meditation to small doses, no more than a couple of minutes, or to leave sitting meditation for a time and do activities that gently foster mindfulness instead.

Sometimes it's the practice or technique that doesn't work for us. We might feel we should stick at it but if we're not getting much out of it, why carry on? The experience is never lost.

It may be that you never settle on one method, drawing on different techniques instead to suit the situation. You might watch the breath when stressed, listen to a self-compassion meditation for comfort, or do a body scan to ease tense muscles. This toolkit approach is more realistic for many of us. We don't have to sit on a mat at a certain time every day for meditation and mindfulness to become part of our daily lives.

13 the pressure of positive thinking

Given the choice, most of us would rather our glass were half full than half empty. A positive approach looks for possibilities. If life gives you lemons, make lemonade.

But it isn't always that easy. Sometimes it's a challenge to turn our thinking around. Staying positive becomes a pressure.

falling foul of the positive police

'You've got to keep positive'. How many of us have heard this or said it ourselves? It's usually at a bad time; someone is dealing with illness or had poor exam results. As if it were that simple.

Most of us fall foul of the Positive Police at some point. It's the insistence on looking for the upside whatever the situation. There's positive or negative with no in between. One is good, the other is bad.

This doesn't allow for natural human emotions like anger, sadness and fear. Take someone whose partner dies suddenly. They might try to focus on the positive, being thankful their loved one died quickly and for the life they had together, but they could be pushing down very normal responses that are part of grieving.

Staying positive at all costs encourages us to put on a front. This can be tiring work and the mask can slip. This is often felt as a failure, making it even harder to stay upbeat. The truth is, we don't always have to turn things around. Sometimes life's lemons are sour and that's how it is. Forget the lemonade.

It's not as if we have stay relentlessly positive to get through tough times. We can fall into the depths, feel beaten, even think of ending our lives, and still survive. In many respects, it's the sinking down and facing our demons that allows us to come back up again.

when rose coloured glasses crack

Positive thinking is full of promises. It isn't our circumstances that holds us back, it's what we believe about ourselves. You can if you think you can.

While there is some truth in this, it's a simplistic formula. Thinking positively about something doesn't mean we'll get the outcome we want. On the morning of a job interview, we visualise ourselves making a great impression on the panel, convinced the job is ours. This doesn't mean we're automatically going to get it. There are numerous factors at play over which we have no control.

Recent research suggests that positive thinking techniques don't work as well as once thought. Gabriele Oettingen from New York University asked students to make a note of how often they fantasised about getting their dream job when they graduated. The students who fantasized the most ended up with fewer job offers and smaller salaries. In another of her studies, women on a weight-reduction programme who imagined the most positive outcomes lost fewer pounds overall.

As Oettingen says: 'Positive thinking fools our minds into perceiving that we've already attained our goal, slackening our readiness to pursue it'. But the answer isn't to go the other way and dwell on the challenges. Oettingen suggests 'mental contrasting', focusing on positive outcomes while considering the obstacles and how to overcome them.

This links to ground-breaking research on optimism in the 1980s by psychologists Michael Sheier and Charles Carver. They found that optimists have better health habits and coping strategies. If they have a serious health condition, they are more likely to make lifestyle choices that promote recovery and rehabilitation. They are also better at accepting what can't be changed, allowing them to move on with their lives. In the words of Sheier, 'Optimists are not simply being Pollyannas; they're problem solvers who try to improve the situation.'

We can repeat self-belief mantras until we're blue in the face. In itself, positive thinking doesn't make things happen.

the shangri-la of happiness

How can I be happy? It's a basic human question that many of us wrestle with. But there's a major flaw with it.

The question presumes that we can be happy all the time. Happiness is the ideal, a glowing yardstick against which everything is measured. But happiness isn't absolute. Like all human emotions, it has its shades and fluctuations, ranging from cheer and contentment to joy and elation.

Likewise, there are grades of unhappiness. We may think our lives are miserable but some days or hours will be less so than others. There may even be short periods of enjoyment and pleasure. We miss these if we're clinging onto misery as something permanent and unchanging.

Perhaps a better question is, how can we be happier? By looking for ways of increasing the activities that give us happy feelings, we might generally feel more contented with ourselves and the world. This approach builds on what is best in our lives. It also understands that what makes us happy shifts many times during our lifetime, shaped by our age, circumstances and experience.

If our ideas about happiness are too fixed, we risk living on future promise. We'll be happy when we meet a partner, when we get a better job, when we've lost weight. But there are no guarantees, and we could spend our lives chasing rainbows.

Not that periods of concern, sadness or upset are such a bad thing. They are part of being human. In many ways, the tough times allow us to savour the happier times. They become brighter from the contrast.

14 the proof of the pudding

The proof of a pudding is in the eating. No matter how delicious it looks, we wouldn't go around telling people how fantastic it was without trying it first. But when it comes to other matters, we can be very quick to give our opinion.

Developing critical thinking encourages us to think before we speak. It helps us understand that even if we might think the pudding is the best we've ever had, ours is just one of many views.

facts before fiction

We're sharing our opinions more than ever before. The increase of social media and internet forums has seen an explosion of armchair pundits. This is exciting in many ways, making for lively debate whether it's politics or what's on TV, but it's a breeding ground for sloppy thinking.

Researching a subject takes time and energy. It's easier to spout off; more so if it's just regurgitating what someone else has said. We live in an age of mis-information where the lines between fact and fiction blur.

A critical thinker approaches this daily bombardment with healthy scepticism. Just because someone writes or says something doesn't automatically make it true. Evidence can be twisted to fit an argument or change as it passes from one person to another, as in the case of gossip. Better to take it all with a pinch of salt.

The pudding analogy reminds us to consider the value of evidence in forming an opinion. If we were building up a picture of a person, we would draw from many sources. There would be the hard facts, like their date of birth and where they went to school, but there would plenty of softer evidence: photographs, letters, their taste in clothes and interests. Even if they wrote a memoir, it wouldn't be the whole story, just their version of events. We'd need to hear what other people had to say about them.

In most cases, it's the combination of different kinds of evidence that gives us the best understanding. Our world is complex. Each of us has an individual perspective wholly unique to us. This makes for millions of viewpoints in which we have to find common ground. Absolute truth is a sticky area, even where processes are rigorous, like science and the law courts.

Appreciating the value of evidence, along with its limitations, is essential to being an effective thinker. If we understand that several, if not numerous, pieces of evidence are needed to get a clearer picture, we're less likely to make snap judgements. It's a guard against unhelpful thinking habits, like generalising ('They always behave like that') or seeing things in black and white.

It can also help us make important decisions. Better to weigh up the situation rather than just diving in and hoping for the best.

the responsibility of free speech

'I disapprove of what you say, but I will defend to the death your right to say it'. These words by Voltaire's biographer, Evelyn Beatrice Hall, hit at the core of free speech. We might disagree with someone's views but they have as much right as us to express them.

But lines have to be drawn. If we really believe that people can say what they like, this means everything. If a child comes home from school crying because they are being called names, they should be told, 'The bullies have every right to call you names and you can do it back'. Likewise, any form of hate crime is acceptable, whether it's racial abuse on social media or homophobic attacks on the streets.

In countries like the UK, there is various legislation restricting what we say and write. This includes libel, slander, copyright violation and the right to privacy. While any system of censorship has its flaws, it helps to protect people.

With the growth of social media, many use it as a platform to express strong, often prejudiced opinion. The worst culprits are the internet trolls, but they are not alone. The relative freedom and anonymity of the internet has created a culture of no holds barred. Every opinion has as much value as the next. The rantings of Joe Bloggs are equal to someone with experience and expertise.

The stock phrase of this world is, 'I'm entitled to my opinion'. It often comes early in an argument – usually after a challenge – and stops the debate in its tracks. The person has their view and that is that; they're not prepared to discuss it. This is usually because their position is easily picked apart.

People think they have the right to say whatever they like without any comeback. Patrick Stokes, an Australian lecturer in Philosophy, tells his students, 'You are not entitled to your opinion, you are only entitled to what you can argue for'. If we're going to express strong opinions, we have to be prepared to make the case for them – and take the consequences. If we're entitled to our opinion, others are too.

when our guts get it wrong

Gut instinct is hardwired into our species. Early humans needed quick and automatic reactions for survival. If a predator appeared, it wouldn't be the time to start having an internal debate about what to do. It was fight or flight.

But our guts make mistakes. Someone might be convinced they have a brain tumour – they just know it – but tests show they are clear. Another marries the person they believe they are meant to be with for the rest of our lives. Two years later, they're divorced.

The reasoning process is often coloured by our gut feelings, especially in emotional matters. These are the ones we 'feel in our bones'; the classic hunch. Of course, our intuition is sometimes right. It's a useful tool, particularly if we need to act quickly. But it may be more informed by our evidence-collecting abilities than we realise. We get the feeling someone is lying to us but we may simply be picking up on the cues effectively.

While there is a place in life for the hunch, the biggest risk with going with our gut is getting it terribly wrong.

clinging on to core beliefs

Our core beliefs allow us to say, This is who I am and this is what I believe. They ground us in ourselves and our communities.

But there's a downside. If we cherish them too much, it makes us quick to dismiss any challenges. We believe we are right, and that is enough. If someone else shares our beliefs, all the better. If it's hundreds and thousands of people, we must be right.

We forget we're products of our time and the society we're born into. While it may be unsettling to think our beliefs are just a matter of chance, it means we're not bound to one mindset or view. We don't have to blindly accept what we've been taught.

Indeed, a critical thinker welcomes alternative opinion. It's an opportunity to test out beliefs. At the end of the day, if they are secure and well-founded, they can take a bit of prodding.

15 no time like the present

Living in the now is a common theme in the mind, body and soul world. It offers a quick solution to our worries and fears. If we become more present in our lives, we will be happier.

But this fast-track to contentment can be elusive. Is it something to aim for all the time, or is it more realistic to find a balance between past, present and future?

now is where it's at

'Life is now. There was never a time when your life was not now, nor will there ever be'. These words from Eckhart Tolle's influential work 'The Power of Now', touch on a basic truth of life: now is where it happens.

But for Tolle and numerous other spiritual teachers and traditions, now isn't where most of us live. We're too caught up in our thoughts; ruminating, planning, anticipating, mulling. If we allowed our attention to rest in the present, we'd no longer dwell on the past or worry about what's to come. We'd fully accept what happens in the now, almost as if we had chosen it.

This has a strong appeal – and no wonder – but it can be challenging in practice. Time may be an illusion but our lives are built around it. We've functioned that way for so long, it can be a struggle to be in the moment for short periods, never mind the radical change that spiritual teachers often promote.

We might be cheering our sports team during a win or struck by a view. For a brief moment, only the present matters and the sense of being and wholeness that gives us. But it's usually temporary. We get a fleeting glimpse before it disappears like a will-o'-the-wisp.

Reading books like 'The Power of Now', we might feel that if we're not living in the now, then we're not really living. We're existing in a half-life, a hamster wheel of never-ending thought. But it's helpful to remember that what Tolle and others put forward is only one way of seeing things. After all, the number of people who live wholly in the moment are probably few and far between.

Perhaps it's more realistic to see it as a skill we can develop to enhance our lives. There doesn't have to be a complete shift; it can sit within our usual way of being in the world.

focusing our thoughts

As we get older, life adds layers, steadily removing us from the direct experience. We lose the immediacy of childhood. The Monkey Mind runs around in all directions, jumping from the past to the future to the present and back again.

There are ways of cutting through this mental clutter. But it takes application, a conscious effort to focus the mind.

We see this with professionals who have honed their ability to concentrate. A surgeon and their team have to be intently focused on the task, aware of each other and what is happening with the patient. A counsellor gives their full attention to a client, responding to what is said in the moment rather than jumping ahead and second guessing. A successful sportsperson doesn't allow themselves to be preoccupied by past failures. The events of the moment are what matter.

Meditation and mindfulness can help develop our attention. When the Monkey Mind wanders, which it does regularly, it is brought back to the focal point, whether the breath or an everyday activity like washing up.

The more we practice, the better we get at it. We become familiar with the tics and tricks of our minds. We're less distracted by the stuff replaying over in our heads and know how to bring ourselves back when we are.

As with any mental discipline, it can be challenging to sustain for prolonged periods. We often need to rest our minds afterwards. The length of time isn't as important as the quality of it; shining a light on the present moment, for however long that is.

savouring the moment

Mindfulness and meditation are usually practiced from a place of neutrality. If we were eating mindfully, we'd notice the taste of the food and our feelings about it – but in a detached way. It wouldn't matter if we liked or enjoyed it.

This can be a stumbling block for some of us. With nothing to hang onto, the Monkey Mind gets restless.

There isn't a rulebook that says you have to remain neutral. If plugging into your curiosity and sense of wonder helps you focus, then do that.

Use your senses to tune in. What can you see, hear, smell, touch and taste? How does that make you feel? Hold emotions like joy, love and thankfulness in your attention. This way, an activity becomes an exploration. You may have done something hundreds of times before, but it becomes a new experience. Your monkey becomes so engrossed, it doesn't wander off.

This approach helps to counter negative states of mind. Life is stuffed with moments to savour – it's being open to them.

diverting the mind

Living in the now applies to all experiences, not just the pleasant ones. This means sitting with states like pain and distress and noticing our responses without engaging in them.

It takes skill and practice to do this. The opposite can happen; the more we try to sit with some states, the worse we feel.

Sometimes we don't want to be in the now, and distraction can be an effective coping strategy. Take a person having hours of medical treatment. They might want it to pass quickly with as little discomfort as possible. Is there really any harm in escaping into a good book or losing themselves in music?

Distraction techniques can be an effective part of our mental toolkit. They allow us to switch off from our troubles, parking them for a time while we soothe or entertain ourselves. This rests the brain and creates distance, so we can come back to problems with fresh eyes.

past, present and future together

Lao-Tzu, ancient Chinese philosopher and writer, is attributed with saying, 'If you are depressed, you are living in the past. If you are anxious, you are living in the future. If you are at peace, you are living in the present'.

Only the present comes well out of such a mindset. Yet the

past and future are an essential part of what makes us human.

While relentlessly chewing over bad experiences isn't good for our mental wellbeing, the past is part of us. Reflection is an integral part of personal growth, and this might mean digging up events from years ago. Sometimes we need to retrace our steps to have a better understanding of who we are and what shaped us. Looking back also allows us to see how far we've come.

If the past isn't important, then heritage and history doesn't matter. But it enriches us so much, not just as individuals but the diverse societies and cultures we live in. It connects us to family and communities, and our younger selves.

When it comes to the future, most of us aren't in a position to live for the day. We have to think about tomorrow and the weeks and months to come. Our choices are often affected by the future: what we do with our money, how we look after our health, the hopes we have for our children. While it isn't helpful to worry unnecessarily about the future, looking ahead motivates us and gives us purpose.

Given that we go through our daily lives with so much reference to the past and the future, is it any wonder that surrendering ourselves to the now might be too much to ask? How many of us could genuinely give up our hold on yesterday and tomorrow? Even if we were to make the shift, it would be challenging within a society that functions in a past-present-future model of life.

An alternative approach is to embrace it all. Rather than seeing past and future as poor cousins to the now, they are part a glorious whole. We can develop our ability to be in the now more fully, to get the most out of this experience called living, but we are also creatures that reflect and reminisce, plan, hope and dream.

16 waking up to enlightenment

The story goes that around two and a half thousand years ago in India, Siddhartha Gautama sat under a tree vowing never to rise until he achieved perfect enlightenment. After days of meditation, he experienced an awakening and was known from that time as the Buddha or the Enlightened One.

A simple story but our understanding of Buddhist enlightenment isn't so straightforward. Even the Buddha found it difficult to put into words. What is enlightenment? Is it a spiritual Shangri-La or something much more everyday and obtainable?

describing the indescribable

People have written about spiritual enlightenment for hundreds of years, but there isn't one definitive description. It's often called the 'indescribable'.

The key feature appears to be a fundamental shift in the perception of reality. Meditation practices strip away layers of thinking until existence is experienced in a pure and direct way. The person reaches a state of being free of thought, sometimes described as a voidness.

Most of us see the world in a solid way. The book or device you are reading this on is a physical object, separate from the other objects around it. We experience ourselves like this – there is 'me' and there is 'you'.

The edges blur for the enlightened person. There's no longer a sense of separation, a division between the self and non-self. The solidness is seen for what it is; an illusion. Perhaps it's like that moment of looking at an optical illusion when another perspective is suddenly revealed. You wonder at not having seen it before when it's so obvious.

Along with this is a letting go of the ego. Or perhaps not so much a letting go as an understanding that it is part of the whole, no more or less important than everything else. This increases compassion; when we are all so interconnected, to hurt another is to hurt ourselves.

This new or perhaps rediscovered clarity is anchored to the

present moment. The enlightened person is awake to the now as it happens and to whatever life offers, not struggling against it or dwelling on the past or future. As Jack Kornfield, American Buddhist, says, '…we do not remove ourselves from life but rest in the very centre of it'. Enlightenment is a homecoming rather than something to be found outside of ourselves.

a journey of awakenings

In Sanskrit, the classical Indian language, the word for enlightenment is 'bodhi', which means 'awakened'. To be a buddha is to be 'one who is awake'.

The idea of an awakening carries with it a sense of instant change. One moment we're asleep, the next awake; eyes wide open, seeing the world as never before. It's an attractive idea, and there are people who approach Buddhism with the hope of this swift transformation. They find a tree, determined to meditate under it until they've reached enlightenment. Few do, of course.

While there are tales of instant Buddhahood, writings suggest it is more of a gradual process; an accumulation of awakenings over a lifetime – or many lifetimes, depending on your beliefs. It wasn't fast-track for the Buddha. By the time he sat under the tree, he had already spent many years exploring yogic meditation and asceticism.

Rather than seeing enlightenment as an absolute state – you're either enlightened or you're not – it may be more helpful to think of it like the word 'knowledge'. It builds on many insights over time.

The philosophical framework behind enlightenment tells us what these insights are. Writers on the subject generally agree that it is waking up to the truth, or the true nature, of our existence. In Buddhism, this is the Four Noble Truths.

The First Noble Truth is the truth of dukkha. Life is suffering. It begins with the pain of birth and never stops. Growing old is dukkha, as is death. We crave and cling on to impermanent states and objects, like money and good health, trying to fulfil our desires on the one hand, while avoiding what we don't want on the other. This is the cause of our unhappiness and is the Second Noble Truth. We don't understand the first truth – this is how life is – and it puts us at odds with our existence.

We end our suffering by letting go of our craving and clinging. This Third Noble Truth is the aim of Buddhist practice.

The Fourth Noble Truth is the way to do this. It's called The Noble Eightfold Path and can be divided into three areas: living in an ethical way, developing wisdom and increasing concentration through meditative practice. The different parts of the path are followed at the same time. But it's the means, not the end. It's the raft that takes us from the ego-bound shore to enlightenment, where it can be discarded.

It usually takes dedication to the Buddhist path to come to a full understanding of the Truths and the change of consciousness this brings. While mind-altering drugs are sometimes used as a quick route to enlightenment, there is a risk of psychosis and other mental health problems. Wiser to spend time like the Buddha under the guidance of teachers, building up the skills and expertise to deal with such a profound mental shift.

the buddhas among us

Considering that Buddhism has been around for over two and a half thousand years, the enlightened being seems to be a rare individual. Of course, there are people who are fond of telling everyone how enlightened they are, but they're often not. They profess to be egoless but are usually narcissistic. Unfortunately, some of them have enough charisma to set themselves up as spiritual gurus and leaders.

We might wonder how to spot an enlightened person. Some people think it's an irrelevant question, but it's only natural to be curious. We might expect them to have a special quality; something in the way they carry themselves in the world that draws people to them. But we're unlikely to come across many enlightened people in our lifetime – and even then, may not know we have.

It seems we might never get the chance to meet a fully enlightened being. Sadhguru from the Isha Foundation talks about how the moment of reaching perfect enlightenment and leaving the body are often the same. The body dies at that instant. Only a very skilful practitioner can keep hold of the body and does this by maintaining some connection to it. He gives the example of the guru who used his love of food. This pegs the person down, so they continue to live and be an inspiration and example to others. This is the Buddhist ideal of the Bodhisattva; someone who postpones full enlightenment to stay on earth for the sake of humankind.

the way or just one way?

The Buddha wasn't a god. When people bow to his figure at shrines, they are honouring the buddha within themselves and the potential for buddhahood that we all have. It's a democratic religion that way; enlightenment isn't just for a special few.

There is the tale of the beggar on the side of the road who has been sitting on a box for thirty years. A stranger encourages him to take a look inside. The box isn't empty as the beggar imagined but full of gold. The parable is that we only need look inside ourselves to awaken to what is already there.

But if it's so close, why can enlightenment feel so out of reach? We might have tantalising glimpses, temporary tears in our reality that allow us to perceive our world in a different way, but often it's like chasing a rainbow within ourselves and never finding the end.

Perhaps the day to day, moment to moment commitment is too much for most of us. It isn't that special powers are needed, it just takes effort. The path requires application, and the discipline of regular meditative practice to achieve a sense of oneness or Samadhi. Not that we should strive for it. Dilgo Khyentse, a Vajrayana master, said, '…there is no need to behave in any special way or attempt to attain anything above and beyond what you actually are'. It's a Buddhist paradox; enlightenment isn't a goal yet it seems to have the demands of one.

Ultimately, the Buddhist path is only one way to live life, not necessarily better than any other. It isn't above criticism.

It can be argued that it has a coolness about it, a detachment from the human experience. It may be true that little can be counted on to bring lasting fulfilment but isn't it possible to be mostly fulfilled? Life isn't just dukkha. It has its joys and marvels, and suffering is the price of love in many ways.

Better to let go of the idea of enlightenment than be frustrated by it. But perhaps that's the idea. As Indian guru, Sri Nisargadatta says, 'There is no such thing as enlightenment. The appreciation of this fact is itself enlightenment'.

17 the interfering ego

The ego gets a bad rap when it comes to spirituality. There it stands, overinflated with its own importance, its demands and trivial concerns keeping us too attached to the material world. But is the ego our enemy? Rather than trying to bash it down, perhaps it needs a tender touch.

doing the self down

The ego gives us a sense of separateness: there is 'me' and there is 'not me'. From a spiritual view, especially Buddhism, this is an illusion. We are all one. The more ego we have, the more we buy into the illusion – and vice versa.

This mindset sees things on a sliding scale. We have the ego maniacs at one end, completely caught up in the physical world and their grandiose beliefs about themselves. As we go through the scale, there is less dependence on the material world and increased wisdom, kindness and selflessness. Finally, we reach full spiritual enlightenment, the ego-free flow and unity between all things.

Within this ideology, believing we are our bodies and minds is the same as holding a jug and saying, This jug is me. To get closer to who we really are, we have to peel back the layers of thought and trappings of physical existence.

It's a view of the self that permeates the mind, spirit and body world – and one that often demonises the ego. It's in the way, a block to be overcome. People set off on a mission to squash it down, or even eradicate it. By subduing the ego and not giving in to its cravings and demands, the spirit will be liberated from the body. Self-mortification is at the extreme, such as fasting for long periods and sleeping on thorns.

Having experienced it himself, the Buddha didn't encourage this hard-line asceticism. His was a 'Middle Way', between abstinence and endurance on one side and the indulgence of sensual pleasures on the other. Even so, we can easily get drawn into self-denial.

This gives the critical voice in our heads a green light. It tells us we're selfish and self-absorbed, too proud or pleased with ourselves. This doesn't help when our inner resources are low, yet this is often the time when we turn to spirituality. Being depressed, anxious, or having poor self-esteem makes us particularly vulnerable to the idea of freeing ourselves from the ego.

But it's incredibly challenging to let go of the concept of self. We chip away to find it clings on harder than ever. It isn't such a surprise; we've functioned that way from being born. Subjectively, a self exists. We have a body that is separate from other bodies, and this body has a brain where we have our thoughts. These tell us we're an individual, a unique 'me' with our personality and quirks. It might be an illusion, but this self-contained way of seeing the world is how we experience it.

There is an alternative, healthier approach; one that builds us up rather than breaking us down. In short, embracing the ego.

embracing the ego

Given that we find ourselves in a body with a subjective self, a different tack is to celebrate our uniqueness. This approach sees the purpose of life as being as much of ourselves as we can be.

Within psychology, this is the theory of self-actualisation. It also has a scale – Maslow's hierarchy of needs, developed in the 1940-50s and expanded in the 1970s. We all have needs to be met, starting at the base of the pyramid with food and shelter and moving through stages of growth – safety, love and belonging; esteem; and cognitive and aesthetic needs – until we reach self-actualisation.

Self-transcendence, at the apex, was a later addition by Maslow. This goes beyond individual needs. The transcended person sees their purpose in the world in relation to other human beings and the positive influence and impact they can have.

Maslow made case studies of historic self-actualisers, like Albert Einstein and Gandhi. Common characteristics include a deep appreciation of basic life experience, resourcefulness and independence, an acceptance of themselves and others, and concern for the welfare of humanity.

This model sees the self as something to be nurtured and developed rather than mastered or dismantled. Better to work on our shortcomings while building on our strengths, talents and potential. Our core nature isn't hiding somewhere inside us; we grow into it. We don't reduce; we become.

18 a random universe

We like to think there is some kind of natural order, that we're not just floating around on a random piece of rock. Whether it's a belief in fate, karma or a fair universe, we're comforted by the idea of wider forces at work. But if we're not careful, it can lead us up the garden path.

destined for disappointment

In the Greek tragedy, Oedipus's life is determined in advance. Unable to escape his destiny, he fulfils the prophecy of killing his father and marrying his mother.

Few of us take such a hard-core approach to fate, but when significant events happen, we might think that destiny had a hand in it. Couples say, 'We were meant to be together', as if the universe or some other force arranged the right conditions, drawing them together irresistibly. This conviction is heightened if coincidence has been at play; teenage sweethearts meeting by accident thirty years later.

Disasters often bring out a sense of fate. A person who misses a fatal flight says, 'I wasn't meant to be on that plane'. But what about the people who were? Were they meant to die?

Fate makes us feel special, that our lives aren't just incidental. The universe may be large but we have our place within it, and our story matters. The downside is the disappointment when events don't go our way. We were destined to be with our partner forever but break up a couple of years down the line. The dream job meant for us goes to someone else.

Too much reliance on outside forces can discourage us from shaping our own destiny. Rather than being written in the stars, we usually have to write our story ourselves.

no rhyme or reason

Everything happens for a reason – or so people say when something bad happens. There has to be a purpose to it, even if it isn't clear at the time.

It's understandable why people think like this, especially in difficult circumstances. It gives meaning to the events in our lives. But it can be a trite comment to make to someone going through tough times. It's like saying that it happened by design. It wasn't just bad luck or accident.

There often isn't any reason. Life can be randomly cruel. This doesn't mean that good can't come out of the worst circumstances, but it's not why they happen in the first place.

living on a prayer

Prayer can be a life-enhancing activity, connecting people to a wider sense of the world and to others in their faith community. It's a way of expressing deep hopes and desires, especially for the wellbeing and happiness of our loved ones.

The risk is that too much expectation is attached to it. Praying becomes a wish-fulfilment exercise.

For every miraculous tale of divine intervention, there are countless others with a different outcome. Why would a higher power save a sick child in one hospital bed but not the other? Who does God go with in a war where both sides pray for victory? Whoever prays the most?

Prayer gives people strength and comfort in trying circumstances, but it can't be depended on to grant wishes. If nothing else, what might be claimed as divine intervention could be something much more down to earth; the work of a dedicated medical team or the grit and determination of an individual – or just chance.

what goes around doesn't always come around

In its simplest form, karma is about reaping what we sow. We have the free will to make choices, but these have consequences. Spread kindness and it will ripple out before coming back to us. Throw out negativity and it will smack us in the face at some point in the future – which might be the next life, if you believe in reincarnation.

Karma is a key concept in some religions. It entered popular culture in the 1960s and tends to be seen in terms of good karma and bad karma, especially the latter. We don't need to take revenge on someone who has treated us badly. Karma will do it for us. Indeed, the karma bus is already heading their way.

It's no surprise that Christian-based societies have shoe-horned karma into a good versus evil scenario. All good actions lead to goodness coming back (reward); all bad actions lead to badness coming back (punishment). It isn't so different to heaven and hell; it just happens during our lifetime rather than after it.

Karma is often seen as some kind of loyalty card. Fill our days with kind actions and thoughts and we'll gain on the investment – or so we hope. It's a shock when it doesn't happen. But being a good person doesn't mean an automatic pay out in the future. Likewise, the bad person might get away with their behaviour. The karma bus could be heading in a different direction – and it may be ours.

Within Buddhist thinking, there is a less simplistic view of karma based around causality. We are all interconnected, and our actions, however small, have consequences; one affects the other in a domino effect.

We're in a supermarket and someone is rude to us. We're so busy dwelling on it during the drive home, we nearly have an accident. The other driver, shaken by the experience, takes it out on their partner when they get home. The partner, a doctor, has a poor night's sleep and isn't as sensitive when delivering bad news to a patient the next morning.

These actions aren't simply good or bad. When we nearly cause a crash, it isn't because we were being 'bad' as such. We just allowed ourselves to get caught up in our thoughts, affecting our concentration.

This approach to karma encourages us to think about the choices we make in the moment. It looks beyond blanket responses like 'I must always be kind' and asks what the best course of action for a particular situation is. A seemingly good deed doesn't always lead to a positive outcome. We dive in to help an elderly person cross the road, but they may have preferred to do it alone as part of keeping independent.

In this view of karma, we only have to concern ourselves with our behaviour. What others do is their business. Moment to moment we exercise a choice about the kind of person we want to be, and our actions shape who we become.

the pseudo-science of the secret

The Law of Attraction came to the fore in 2006 with Rhonda Byrne's film 'The Secret', closely followed by a book of the same name. It's based on the idea that 'like attracts like'. Whatever happens to us in our lives is as a result of what we have attracted into it. According to Byrne, 'You are the one who calls the Law of Attraction into action, and you do it through your thoughts'.

The Secret tells us our thinking is far more powerful than we realise. If we send out thoughts on a positive frequency, we attract positive energy back to us – and vice versa. Our thoughts are like magnets, so potent we manifest whatever we desire for ourselves. The universe is a genie, granting our wishes.

The trick is acting as if we already have what we want. This means creating powerful thoughts in the present tense. If the universe hears the repeated thought 'I want to be rich', it gives us back the state of wanting. If we send out 'I am rich', the thought becomes reality. This is turbo-charged if we give gratitude in advance.

These ideas are brought together in the book 'The Secret', the Law of Attraction's bible. It's deliberately tantalizing, with its seal and antique font with the words, 'You hold in your hands a great secret'. It's as if we have stumbled across ancient wisdom and are one of the chosen few that it will be imparted to.

Once we break the seal and start reading, we're told there is a law of the universe that has been in place since the beginning of time. It can be found in religions and cultures through the ages and will affect our entire life experience from the cradle to the grave.

The book has a veneer of academic credibility, as if it has been a scholarly labour gathering all the evidence in one place. We are reassured that Galileo, Einstein and other notable thinkers knew about the Law of Attraction. It's even compatible with quantum physics. With such an abundance of proof, how can we doubt it?

It is this pseudo-scientific aspect that has brought most criticism. There isn't a Law of Attraction in quantum physics.

The energy fields emitted from our brains are too small to have any effect on the physical world around us, never mind control what happens to us. From a scientific point of view, it's nonsense.

Still, it's an intriguing concept and we might be tempted to try it. But then we don't get the job we wanted, our soul mate doesn't appear and we're broke as ever. We pore over The Secret, trying to work out what it is we're doing wrong, blaming ourselves for not believing it enough. If we attract everything into our lives, then it's our own fault if we're ill or tragedy strikes.

Ultimately the Law of Attraction encourages us to believe in magic; that words are spells with the power to alter physical reality. Of course, there are people who say it worked for them but that is probably more to do with positive thinking and luck.

the fallacy of fairness

At some point in our childhoods, we all cried out, 'It's not fair!'. Whether it was having to go to bed early or being first out in a party game, it seemed that life was out to spoil our fun.

The feeling can be just as strong when we're older; more so with the added complexity that adulthood brings. We come off worst in a divorce settlement, bear the brunt of an elderly parent's demands or lose out in a promotion. Life gives us lemons, and they're tart to the taste.

Someone gets diagnosed with a serious health condition and thinks, why me? They've lived a good life, unlike so-and-so who's caused so much trouble. Why didn't it happen to them?

The real question is, why not me? Life is indiscriminate. It doesn't work on the basis of bad things only happen to bad people.

When we're young, we're told to share our toys and sweets, and it's the taking part that counts in sport. These important teachings nurture a sense of equality – we're all special – but life doesn't play that way. We're not clocking up a tally that gets re-jigged to make sure everyone gets their fair share.

The problem with 'It's not fair!' is that it encourages self-pity. If we're not careful, we become stuck in the groove of 'Poor me!'. This stops us looking for potential solutions. Take a sportsperson who has some skill but lacks the talent of others in the same field. They could wallow in their short-comings or work out a way of developing their abilities to the fullest.

Of course, there are injustices that need to be addressed, but better to do something about it than sitting around bemoaning the world. Even so, we have to be realistic. We might expect the justice system to be fair but sometimes it lets us down. Life isn't a Hollywood film. It won't always work out in our favour, even when right is on our side.

you should be so lucky

We all like the idea of good luck. It's the sense of possibility. Fortune might smile on us like a beam of sunshine.

Unlike fate or a belief in divine intervention, we know that luck is just random events that happen to work our favour. This means there's always a chance of cheating probability, even when the odds are stacked against us.

Although some people seem to have a lucky star above their heads, luck doesn't discriminate and that's what makes it so appealing. Some individuals may start off with more advantages than others but fortunes can change – and vice versa.

You may believe you increase your good fortune by wearing or carrying charms. But chances are you make your own luck. As humourist R E Shay is credited with saying, 'Depend on the rabbit's foot if you will, but remember, it didn't work for the rabbit'.

19 another fine mess

It isn't just Stan and Ollie who find themselves in messy situations. Everyday living is untidy. This can be challenging, especially if we like things to be neat and in place. The question is, is there a way of going with the flow rather than fighting against it? Perhaps even finding calm in the chaos?

going with the flow

Human life is messy. Freshly laundered clothes get dirty, dust collects and settles, and new things lose their shine. It all makes for daily irritations: the car breaks down, our mobile phone plays up, and we have to see the dentist about a painful tooth. It hits us in the pocket and spoils our plans.

Relationships are one of the messiest aspects of our lives. Love doesn't always mean harmony.

In the wider world, life for many is chaotic and unstable, affected by wars, natural disasters and poverty.

The fact is, we live in houses of sand. But how many of us put our heads in the sand and pretend differently?

If we treat life like a garden that has to be beautifully manicured, we have to put a lot of effort into maintaining it. Even so, problems are inevitable. Because that's how life is. No matter how much we try to impose order, there is only so much we can control.

Accepting the essential messiness of life makes it easier. We expect difficulties to crop up; it's a bonus if they don't.

One way of doing this is to change our mindset. Rather than thinking, 'I hope nothing goes wrong', we can alter it to, 'Something may well go wrong but hopefully it won't matter over all'. In most cases, things still get done despite the obstacles and setbacks.

Loosening our hold helps us live with unpredictability. Events won't always go our way, however much planning and preparation we've put in. More effort doesn't guarantee more security. Life goes off at tangents and can turn pear-shaped in an instant.

Of course, it's challenging when events turn our lives upside down. It makes us crave certainty where there is none or very little. The family whose home is flooded want to know when they can move back in and get back to normal. The person with a cancer diagnosis struggles with what the future holds.

But thrashing against wider forces over which we have no control wastes valuable energy. We can still create some order for ourselves – and often need to do this so we don't feel like flotsam or feathers on the wind – but it's understanding that it's within parameters, and those might change.

Sometimes we have to let ourselves be carried along. This allows us to be more flexible and adaptable, key features of resilience.

calm in the chaos

Whether it's a haven at home or the quiet of a temple or forest, pockets of calm are good for the soul in this chaotic world. But we can become too reliant on this kind of environment; inner peace only comes with outer peace. Once we're in this mindset, noise and activity automatically means disturbance and agitation.

We can challenge the idea that our external and internal worlds need to tally.

If you're quick to notice the negative effects of a busy environment, try to be aware of those times when you're too absorbed or content to care. The irony is, we can be most at odd with ourselves in peaceful settings. We escape to the countryside or a place of worship, only to find our problems come into sharp relief once the hustle and bustle drops away.

Try calming your mind when you're out and about. You might be on the bus, in the local park or a coffee shop. You don't need to sit in a meditative posture or close your eyes, just do it on the go. You're likely to get distracted, but with practice you can re-train your mind. Keep feeding in the message that you can feel tranquil whatever your external circumstances.

Another approach is to reduce reliance on rituals and trappings. If you always burn candles when you meditate, leave them unlit. If you practise relaxation techniques at night with the curtains closed, try them in the morning with the curtains open.

As the Buddha said, 'Peace comes from within, do not seek it without'.

cracks of gold

As human beings, we can get hung up on perfection. We take such delight in clean sheets, undisturbed snow or a newborn's fingers. We chase perfect moments and experiences. But they all pass, leaving us with a sense of loss and yearning.

We tend to see perfection in an absolute way, as something fixed and unchanging. In reality, it's much more fluid. Perfection isn't a rigid benchmark that applies on every occasion. Much of it is down to the society and era we live in. Even where there is general consensus – a rock guitarist, say, who is considered one of the best of their generation – some will say a certain track was perfect, others that it was a particular album.

It isn't as if something has to be completely perfect for us to appreciate it as such. Most experiences have shortcomings. We just don't notice them or they're not big enough to matter. Sometimes they even contribute. Take a brilliant singer who goes wrong at the start of a song. The way they deal with it in the moment can become part of an unforgettable performance.

Being a perfectionist means rarely being satisfied. There will always be some fault or other, and when perfection is the bar these become magnified. This makes it hard to take enjoyment in our endeavours. But our failings don't have to hinder us. In many respects, it's the daring to make mistakes that allows us to achieve.

Idealistic expectations often raise their head in spiritual approaches to life. We might aspire to be in a state of inner calm for most, if not all, the time. We adopt a monk-like air, moving slowly and speaking in hushed tones. But then we get irritated, bicker with a family member or feel frustrated. Now we've let ourselves down, which gives us another stick to beat ourselves with.

Few of us are paragons of peace. Most of us get ruffled at some point or other; it goes with the human experience. Life is messy – and that applies as much to our emotional life as the other parts of it, if not more so.

In the Japanese art known as kintsugi, the cracks in a damaged ceramic are repaired with powdered gold. Rather than something to hide, the breakage becomes part of the history of the object. Forget perfection – better to celebrate who we are, cracks and all.

20 it's a wonder-full life

Being curious is one of the best things about being human. It creates new neural connections and helps to keep the brain young. Challenging our ideas about the world frees our thinking, so we don't become too rigid and narrow-minded.

This last chapter celebrates the joy of asking questions – without expecting answers.

a world of wow

When we're children, we're told magical stories. These weave their spell on us and give us a taste for the marvellous. It's exciting to think there are mysterious and supernatural forces at work in the world, taking us beyond the everyday experience.

One of the hardest things about growing up is leaving magic behind. Many of us never do completely. It's harmless in most cases – like suspending disbelief when we go to the theatre – but it can lead us up the garden path. A bereaved person finds themselves manipulated by a supposed psychic or an ill person pins too much hope on an obscure therapy.

Much of what people describe as magical and miraculous can be explained rationally. Despite this, we may cling on to the idea that unseen powers can influence events, even when presented with evidence to the contrary. It's like going to see a magician and believing it is actually magic rather than illusion.

In the end, we don't need magic to be filled with wonder.

Getting into nature is one of the easiest and most effective ways of inspiring amazement in the world around us. It doesn't have to be far; our own gardens and local parks are full of small wonders. When we become attuned to the detail – an insect travelling across a leaf or the way light behaves – we're reminded that nothing is still, the natural world is constantly changing.

It's the same with our bodies. We're incredible creatures. Did you know that every atom in our bodies is billions of years old? Or that if your arteries, veins and capillaries were laid to end to end they would wrap around the world nearly four times? Or that we are mostly empty space? If it was removed from our bodies, the entire human race would fit inside a square the size of a sugar cube!

Discover what stirs you – whether it's science, history, music or any of the marvellous things this world holds - and re-boot your sense of wonder. Tapping into that can be more magical than anything.

the freedom in not knowing

The desire for clear-cut answers is a powerful drive and one of the reasons so many of us turn to religion. We want someone to tell us, This is how it is and this is the way to live your life. But no one knows the answers to life's big questions. Some people think they do, but they can't say with certainty.

In this absence of definite answers, there is something to be said for learning to live with not knowing. This isn't letting go of the search for answers – it still goes on – but it's accepting we may never reach our individual 'Eureka!' moment.

Embracing the unknown opens up our world. We learn that we can look at things in many different ways, even hold a number of perspectives at the same time. Rather than narrowing as we age, and becoming increasingly rigid in our views, we can widen into wisdom. In the words of physicist Richard Feynman: '…it's much more interesting to live not knowing than to have answers which might be wrong'.

The truth may be that our universe, and beyond it, is much more profound and marvellous than we could ever begin to imagine. It's the search that gives our lives purpose. As a character in Kiriakakis' cartoon 'A Day at the Park' says, 'Maybe having all the answers is like wishing for the end of all meaning'.

acknowledgements

Thanks to family and friends, especially Ma, Scott and Ernest, who always believed I'd do something with my writing.

Thanks to Tilla Brook who I was lucky enough to have as a coach and to Bernie Shepherd for our exploratory conversations. I learned so much from both of you.

Thank you to the many authors whose books fired my curiosity and to all the retreat leaders, yoga teachers, counsellors, complementary therapists, and other spiritual and psychological practitioners I have come across over the years. I couldn't have written this book without that experience and learning.

In my working life, I have supported people affected by long-term health conditions. I thank them for the insight their stories have given me. The book wouldn't be the same without it.

Finally, thank you to the writers on the internet who have shared their experience of self-publishing. Your guidance has shown me the way.

afterword

Thank you for finding your way to the *soul survival guide*.

It's the kind of book that becomes known by word of mouth. Please tell people about it. Writing reviews is one way of doing this and can help others decide if the book is for them. You can do this on Amazon and sites like Goodreads.

The book doesn't end here. Join *soul survival guide* on social media and find out more on the website.

facebook: soul survival guide
twitter: ali davenport @soulsurvguide
www.linkedin.com/in/alidavenport

www.soulsurvivalguide.co

45301753R00065

Printed in Poland
by Amazon Fulfillment
Poland Sp. z o.o., Wrocław